X-RAY

D0994273

INTER-VARSITY PRESS
38 De Montfort Street, Leicester LE1 7GP, England

First published under the title X-RAY in a limited edition in 1999

This edition published in 2000

British Library Cataloguing in Publication Data

A catalogue record for this book is available from the British Library.

ISBN 0–85111–520–9

Set in Joanna, Myriad, Letter Gothic, Orator and Synchro
Printed in Great Britain by The Guernsey Press Co. Ltd, Guernsey, Channel Islands.

Inter-Varsity Press is the book-publishing division of the Universities and Colleges Christian Fellowship (formerly the Inter-Varsity Fellowship), a student movement linking Christian Unions in universities and colleges throughout Great Britain , and a member movement of the International Fellowship of Evangelical Students. For more information about local and national activities write to UCCF, 38 De Montfort Street, Leicester LE1 7GP.

Design and Illustration: Paul Airy

Inter-Varsity Press

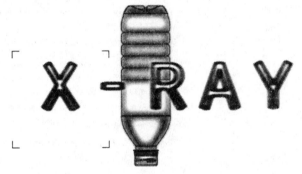

X-RAY

[THE GOSPEL OF JOHN]

FROM THE NEW INTERNATIONAL VERSION OF THE BIBLE

[IN-SIGHT FROM OUTSIDE]

PAUL WESTON

CONTENTS

[THE GOSPEL OF JOHN]

FROM THE NEW INTERNATIONAL VERSION

[IN-SIGHT FROM OUTSIDE]

PAUL WESTON

'THE WORD'

John hits us immediately with huge concepts, intriguing and engaging us. Who or what is this 'Word'? What lies behind the universe? The Word was a concept the people of the first century recognized. For some this was the principle of order in the universe, or the idea of a life force. For Jews it was God speaking, with the power to bring about all that he said. John fills the idea with new meaning. 'The Word' is a person, but more than a human. Jesus Christ is the answer to the big questions.

CHAPTER [1]

[THE GOSPEL OF JOHN]

The Word became flesh

[1]In the beginning was the Word, and the Word was with God, and the Word was God. [2]He was with God in the beginning.

[3]Through him all things were made; without him nothing was made that has been made. [4]In him was life, and that life was the light of all people. [5]The light shines in the darkness, but the darkness has not understood it.

[6]There came a man who was sent from God; his name was John. [7]He came as a witness to testify concerning that light, so that through him all might believe. [8]He himself was not the light; he came only as a witness to the light. [9]The true light that gives light to everyone was coming into the world.

[10]He was in the world, and though the world was made through him, the world did not recognise him. [11]He came to that which was his own, but his own did not

Introduction

What kind of book is John's Gospel?

The Gospel of John, which forms the substance of the book in your hands, is, in many ways, hard to categorize.

Unlike a textbook, it doesn't set out to supply us with lots of information, though of course we will learn new things by reading it.

Unlike a novel, it doesn't project itself as a story which need not be true, but which none the less aims to involve us both intellectually and emotionally. On the contrary, though it is clearly a story with a narrative structure, John's Gospel frequently makes claims precisely at the level of 'truth' – not only in what it writes about, but in the demands it makes upon the reader's life.[1]

I suppose that, formally, it is more like what we would call a 'biography'. After all, John sets out to tell us about another person's life: that of Jesus Christ, born and raised in the region of Galilee in the first century and put to death in Jerusalem around the year AD 30. Even at this level, however, John doesn't tell us a great deal – unlike Matthew and Luke, for example, who tell us more about the circumstances surrounding his birth and early life. John's formal account of Jesus' life begins in the second half of chapter 1, when Jesus is already an adult and has started out on his public work.

This is not to say that John is not interested in what went before Jesus' adulthood. The very first words of the book confirm this big time: 'In the beginning …' These are words

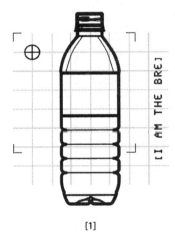

[I AM THE BRE]

[1]

John the Baptist, who appears several times (chapters 1 and 3) before disappearing from view, is not John, the author of this book. A distant relative of Jesus Christ, his main role, like some royal official, was to prepare the way for Jesus' arrival. Many believed that God was about to send a special messenger (the Christ or Messiah). The spotlight fell on John, the dynamic preacher, as he urged baptism as a sign of turning from sin. Was he the promised one? John's answer is unequivocal – he was only a forerunner.

receive him. [12]Yet to all who received him, to those who believed in his name, he gave the right to become children of God – [13]children born not of natural descent, nor of human decision or a husband's will, but born of God.

[14]The Word became flesh and made his dwelling among us. We have seen his glory, the glory of the One and Only, who came from the Father, full of grace and truth. [15]John testifies concerning him. He cries out, saying, 'This was he of whom I said, "He who comes after me has surpassed me because he was before me."' [16]From the fulness of his grace we have all received one blessing after another. [17]For the law was given through Moses; grace and truth came through Jesus Christ. [18]No-one has ever seen God, but God the One and Only, who is at the Father's side, has made him known.

John the Baptist denies being the Christ

[19]Now this was John's testimony when the Jews of Jerusalem sent priests and Levites to ask him who he was. [20]He did not fail to confess, but confessed freely, 'I am not the Christ.'

[21]They asked him, 'Then who are you? Are you Elijah?'

He said, 'I am not.'

'Are you the Prophet?'

He answered, 'No.'

[22]Finally they said, 'Who are you? Give us an answer to take back to those who sent us. What do you say about yourself?'

[23]John replied in the words of Isaiah the prophet, 'I am the voice of one calling in the desert, "Make straight the way for the Lord."'

[24]Now some Pharisees who had been sent [25]questioned him, 'Why then do you baptise if you are not the Christ, nor Elijah, nor the Prophet?'

[26]'I baptise with water,' John replied, 'but among you stands one you do not know. [27]He is the one who comes after me, the thongs of whose sandals I am not worthy to untie.'

that have started many a book, but what sets John's story apart from standard biographical introductions is that the 'beginning' he writes about here is not the hero's birth – with information and background about his family and social context – but rather the beginning of time itself. It's as if the only way that he can adequately introduce Jesus to the reader is by putting him in the global context of eternity and to begin his story at the start of time! For this reason alone, John's Gospel is clearly something more than a standard biography.

Another unusual feature of this 'biography' is that a great deal more space is taken up with its hero's death than would ever be the case with an ordinary biography. You'd get an odd reaction from your publisher if you said that you intended to spend over a third of the biography concentrating on the events surrounding the subject's death. Most biographies describe the subject's death as a way of rounding off the story of his or her life. Rather an obvious point, I grant you, but one which is worth making simply to draw out the contrast between standard biographies and this one.

For here, the subject of Jesus' death takes up the best part of eight chapters, which – when your 'publisher' has only given you twenty-one to play with – is rather excessive. Actually, the last two chapters of the book do not strictly concern his death. But they serve to emphasize the difference, for they are about what Christians refer to as Jesus' 'resurrection': his coming back to life (or – more accurately – his 'passing through' the barrier of death) after being put to death by crucifixion. More of this later.

No wonder then that this book doesn't quite fit under the heading 'biography'. In fact, a new category of writing had to be defined to do justice to what John had written: the name 'gospel'.

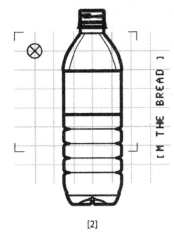

[I'M THE BREAD]

[2]

LAMB OF GOD

Calling Jesus 'the Lamb of God' had an immediate impact. The people would have traced the idea back into their history, in which animal sacrifice played a central part. They knew well the ritual of providing a lamb from their flocks for sacrifice. These sacrifices were given to deal with their dislocated relationship with God. In identifying Jesus as 'the Lamb of God', already John is pointing to Jesus as a sacrifice. He 'takes away the sin of the world' because his sacrifice will be on behalf of others.

[28]This all happened at Bethany on the other side of the Jordan, where John was baptising.

Jesus the Lamb of God

[29]The next day John saw Jesus coming towards him and said, 'Look, the Lamb of God, who takes away the sin of the world! [30]This is the one I meant when I said, "A man who comes after me has surpassed me because he was before me." [31]I myself did not know him, but the reason I came baptising with water was that he might be revealed to Israel.'

[32]Then John gave this testimony: 'I saw the Spirit come down from heaven as a dove and remain on him. [33]I would not have known him, except that the one who sent me to baptise with water told me, "The man on whom you see the Spirit come down and remain is the one who will baptise with the Holy Spirit." [34]I have seen and I testify that this is the Son of God.'

Jesus' first disciples

[35]The next day John was there again with two of his disciples. [36]When he saw Jesus passing by, he said, 'Look, the Lamb of God!'

[37]When the two disciples heard him say this, they followed Jesus. [38]Turning round, Jesus saw them following and asked, 'What do you want?'

They said, 'Rabbi' (which means Teacher), 'where are you staying?'

[39]'Come,' he replied, 'and you will see.'

So they went and saw where he was staying, and spent that day with him. It was about the tenth hour.

[40]Andrew, Simon Peter's brother, was one of the two who heard what John had said and who had followed Jesus. [41]The first thing Andrew did was to find his brother Simon and tell him, 'We have found the Messiah' (that is, the Christ). [42]And he brought him to Jesus.

Jesus looked at him and said, 'You are Simon son of John. You will be called Cephas' (which, when translated, is Peter).

Why John's 'Gospel'?

The word 'gospel' comes from a Greek word literally meaning 'good news'. It was the word used in everyday Greek to describe any 'good' piece of public news: a family birth, a victory in battle, and so on. It was also already in use by Christians contemporary with John for describing in Greek certain events in the Old Testament, but its use to describe a book is new to his work – alongside those of Matthew, Mark and Luke. It characterizes a new kind of writing for, like the other 'Gospels', John's work is obviously written to pass on 'good news'.

The author puts this very clearly towards the end of the book. In 20:30–31 he explains that 'Jesus did many other miraculous signs in the presence of his disciples, which are not recorded in this book. But these are written that you may believe that Jesus is the Christ, the Son of God, and that by believing you may have life in his name.'

John's aim in writing is therefore not simply to inform the reader about the life of its subject (though of course it does do this). Nor is it to engage the imagination (though it does this too). It is rather to expose us to the truth that is embodied in this man Jesus in such a way as to change our minds about him and to transform our entire outlook on life as a result of 'believing' Jesus.

And throughout the history of its publication, John's 'Gospel' has done just that. It has stretched and challenged, stimulated and refocused the minds and lives of an enormous number of readers. But more than that, it has led many to what can only be described as 'a personal encounter' with Jesus Christ that has changed their lives.

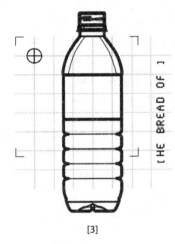

[3]

Encountering life

A couple of years ago I was the main speaker at a week of events exploring Christianity at

Jesus calls Philip and Nathanael

43The next day Jesus decided to leave for Galilee. Finding Philip, he said to him, 'Follow me.'

44Philip, like Andrew and Peter, was from the town of Bethsaida. 45Philip found Nathanael and told him, 'We have found the one Moses wrote about in the Law, and about whom the prophets also wrote – Jesus of Nazareth, the son of Joseph.'

46'Nazareth! Can anything good come from there?' Nathanael asked.

'Come and see,' said Philip.

47When Jesus saw Nathanael approaching, he said of him, 'Here is a true Israelite, in whom there is nothing false.'

48'How do you know me?' Nathanael asked.

Jesus answered, 'I saw you while you were still under the fig-tree before Philip called you.'

49Then Nathanael declared, 'Rabbi, you are the Son of God; you are the King of Israel.'

50Jesus said, 'You believe because I told you I saw you under the fig-tree. You shall see greater things than that.' 51He then added, 'I tell you the truth, you shall see heaven open, and the angels of God ascending and descending on the Son of Man.'

Cambridge University. I decided that each evening's presentation would be a simple public reading of part of John's Gospel followed by an explanation of what that passage might mean for us today. On the final night, the reading was the whole of chapter 20, with its description of the aftermath of Jesus' resurrection, and its effect on his disciples. As I read, I was unaware that somewhere in the audience a student began weeping. He was not your obviously emotional type: he played rugby and was over six feet tall. But he explained to me afterwards that, while nothing in my talk had particularly struck him ('Thanks, pal,' I thought), the moment I started reading the chapter from John, something 'came together' at the centre of his mind and heart that made him recognize who Jesus is. 'I realized that he is everything I have been searching for,' he explained. It is difficult to explain such a response. I cannot 'rationalize' it for you, nor would I want to. There was no emotional pressure being applied, simply a public reading. But somehow there was an encounter between this man and something 'beyond' his experience which made him reach out and grasp the truth that is Jesus Christ. 'These things are written that you may have life …' writes John.

[R E A L   L I V E S]

In this book, you can read about the first-hand experiences of several people who – in different and unique ways – have also come to believe that Jesus is the Christ and have 'received life' in his name. Each has found in Jesus Christ the answer to his or her quest for truth. I invite you to read them for yourself.

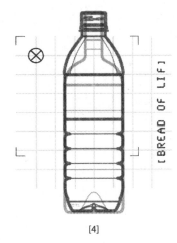

[BREAD OF LIF]

[4]

MIRACLES

John selects seven representative miracles of Jesus in chapters 2 – 11:

- Changing water into wine
- Healing a boy close to death
- Healing a disabled man
- Feeding over 5,000 people
- Walking on water
- Healing a blind man
- Bringing a dead man back to life

These miracles are not there simply to create a sensation. They act as 'signs', pointing beyond the immediate dramatic effect in order to help us reflect on who Jesus Christ is. They did not have automatic effect (see 12:9) because they call for a response not of astonishment, but of recognition.

CHAPTER [2]

Jesus changes water to wine

¹On the third day a wedding took place at Cana in Galilee. Jesus' mother was there, ²and Jesus and his disciples had also been invited to the wedding. ³When the wine was gone, Jesus' mother said to him, 'They have no more wine.'

⁴'Dear woman, why do you involve me?' Jesus replied, 'My time has not yet come.'

⁵His mother said to the servants, 'Do whatever he tells you.'

⁶Nearby stood six stone water jars, the kind used by the Jews for ceremonial washing, each holding from twenty to thirty gallons.

⁷Jesus said to the servants, 'Fill the jars with water'; so they filled them to the brim.

⁸Then he told them, 'Now draw some out and take it to the master of the banquet.'

They did so, ⁹and the master of the banquet tasted the water that had been turned into wine. He did not realise where it had come from, though the servants who had drawn the water knew. Then he called

The purpose of this bit of the book

For my part, in the pages that follow I have tried to introduce some of the themes that John writes about and have tried to show how they relate to some of the 'big' issues in our contemporary lives. I hope you find – like me – that what was written so long ago has an extraordinarily contemporary feel to it.

But, most importantly, I want to invite you to read John's Gospel for yourself. That is the most important part of this book. Skip my stuff if you're pushed for time, and get straight to the words that John wrote. For here is life.

[R E A L   L I V E S]

MARK CHATFIELD

Mark is in his second year of studying maths at university, and also plays cricket for his University 2nd XI team.

Jesus this, Jesus that. I'd heard it all before, but to be honest it'd gone in one ear and out the other. Jesus claimed to be the Son of God – I knew that. So what? I'd never found church the slightest bit interesting and I certainly couldn't see God with my own eyes. How could a man who died 2,000 years ago still be alive today? And yet during Freshers' Week of 1998 it stuck home that Christians really

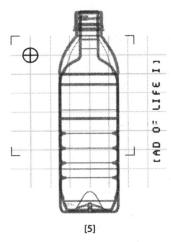

[5]

THE TEMPLE

The Passover was an annual religious festival celebrated to commemorate the deliverance of the people of Israel from slavery in Egypt, a millennium and a half earlier.

The temple in Jerusalem was the established worship centre of the Jewish faith. In order for worshippers to bring animals for sacrifice, they were required to purchase them in the temple precincts. This monopoly allowed greatly inflated prices for the animals. Jesus responds in anger toward this injustice, which contradicted the temple's purpose.

the bridegroom aside ¹⁰and said, 'Everyone brings out the choice wine first and then the cheaper wine after the guests have had too much to drink; but you have saved the best till now.'

¹¹This, the first of his miraculous signs, Jesus performed at Cana in Galilee. He thus revealed his glory, and his disciples put their faith in him.

Jesus clears the temple

¹²After this he went down to Capernaum with his mother and brothers and his disciples. There they stayed for a few days.

¹³When it was almost time for the Jewish Passover, Jesus went up to Jerusalem. ¹⁴In the temple courts he found people selling cattle, sheep and doves, and others sitting at tables exchanging money. ¹⁵So he made a whip out of cords, and drove all from the temple area, both sheep and cattle; he scattered the coins of the money-changers and overturned their tables. ¹⁶To those who sold doves he said, 'Get these out of here! How dare you turn my Father's house into a market!'

¹⁷His disciples remembered that it is written, 'Zeal for your house will consume me.'

were deadly serious about a living Jesus. The guest speaker at a Christian Union event delivered a thought-provoking speech, and afterwards I took the opportunity to chat to him about his faith. Over the next week he and I met on several occasions. I looked objectively at the primary sources for perhaps the first time, and one night, after being convicted of the truth of Jesus' claims, I decided to follow him whole-heartedly.

For nineteen years I had chosen to hide from Christianity. It seemed the easiest option and it meant that I could live my life my own way. I thought I had freedom and that I could find true happiness my way.

But now I can see just how wrong I was. I had not even begun to experience what it really means to live. Since Jesus became the centre of my life, I have been filled to overflowing with real joy and with true peace and with incomparable freedom. The emptiness I once felt in my more reflective moments has been smashed to pieces. My life now has real meaning. I wake up every morning aware of God's amazing love and with the knowledge that one day all our tears will be washed away.

You may have heard it all before. My friends certainly have! And perhaps, like them, you've seen the difference that faith in Jesus Christ makes in our lives. But you're still reading at this point, which suggests that you're intrigued, if only slightly. So why not be

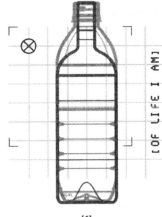

[OF LIFE I AM]

[6]

18Then the Jews demanded of him,

'What miraculous sign can you show us to prove your authority to do all this?'

19Jesus answered them,

'Destroy this temple, and I will raise it again in three days.'

20The Jews replied, 'It has taken forty-six years to build this temple, and you are going to raise it in three days?' 21But the temple he had spoken of was his body. 22After he was raised from the dead, his disciples recalled what he had said. Then they believed the Scripture and the words that Jesus had spoken.

23Now while he was in Jerusalem at the Passover Feast, many people saw the miraculous signs he was doing and believed in his name. 24But Jesus would not entrust himself to them, for he knew all people. 25He did not need human testimony about them, for he knew what was in people.

brave and go and look into Jesus' claims for yourself? Perhaps then, you might come to share in the same rejoicing that thousands of millions around you also share in today.

[1] Where do I start?

'... I must remind myself we are living creatures – we have religious impulses – we must – and yet into what cracks do these impulses flow in a world without religion? It is something I think about every day. Sometimes I think it is the only thing I should be thinking about.'[1]
DOUGLAS COUPLAND

The religious quest

The quest for religious 'truth', for 'reality' – call it what you will – is as old as the hills, even for those such as Coupland who want to believe that we live 'after God' but who still experience what he calls 'religious impulses'. I suppose we either ignore these and pretend they don't exist, or else we are obliged to explore the 'religious dimension'. Perhaps you have never done this before. Well, now's as good a time as any to start.

But where do we start? In the immortal words of Julie Andrews (aka Maria von Trapp of *The Sound of Music* fame), 'Let's start at the very beginning, a very good place to start.' You have in your hands a book that claims to provide answers to the most basic questions about God and about human identity. It too starts at the 'very beginning'.

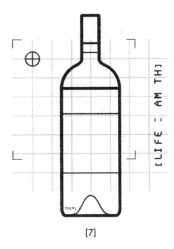

[7]

THE KINGDOM OF GOD

Many Jewish people of the time had their hopes pinned on God intervening in the world to remove evil, and to establish justice, truth and peace. The idea of the 'kingdom of God' encapsulated what it would mean to live under this perfect rule of God. Jesus saw this reign as beginning now, when people are born 'of water and the Spirit'. These images communicate two things: cleansing and renewal. 'Water' provides the picture of washing away impurity, 'Spirit' the life of God coming to transform people inwardly.

CHAPTER [3]

Jesus teaches Nicodemus

¹Now there was a Pharisee named Nicodemus, a member of the Jewish ruling council. ²He came to Jesus at night and said, 'Rabbi, we know you are a teacher who has come from God. For you could not perform the miraculous signs you are doing if God were not with you.'

³In reply Jesus declared, 'I tell you the truth, no-one can see the kingdom of God without being born again.'

⁴'How can anyone be born in old age?' Nicodemus asked. 'Surely they cannot enter a second time into their mother's womb to be born!'

⁵Jesus answered, 'I tell you the truth, no-one can enter the kingdom of God without being born of water and the Spirit. ⁶Flesh gives birth to flesh, but the Spirit gives birth to spirit. ⁷You should not be surprised at my saying, "You must be born again." ⁸The wind blows wherever it pleases. You hear its sound, but you cannot tell where it comes from or where it is going. So it is with

The voice from outside

> *In the beginning was the Word and the Word was with God.*
> JOHN 1:1

As someone whose job it is to try to communicate the Christian message to others, I meet two main reactions to the idea of 'God' among those who have begun to think about him. The first is the reaction that runs along the lines: 'I wish that whoever – or whatever – "god" is, he would let me know what he is like.' The philosopher Bertrand Russell expressed this thought in his *Autobiography* in the following despairing words: 'The centre of me is always and eternally a terrible pain – a curious and wild pain – searching for something beyond what the world contains, something transfigured and infinite – the beatific vision – God – I do not find it, I do not think it is to be found – but the love of it is my life – it's like passionate love for a ghost.'[2]

Perhaps the search today is becoming even more confusing. Where is 'reality' today in our multi-functional, techno-wizardry world? Has it brought us closer to reality, or only to a 'virtual' reality? Describing the experience of 'surfing' the net, one writer puts it this way:

> *Surfing the net is the ultimate postmodern experience. Facing your SVGA display – low radiation/anti-static – poised over the multimedia controls, you launch into new forms of spatiality created by flows of electric information … Reality is soft, malleable, permeable, and available only through the constant discharge of electronic energy signalling across the cosmos … In this land of fantasy and ceaseless journeying, this experience of tasting, sampling, and passing on, truth, knowledge, and facts are all only dots of light on a screen, evanescent, consumable.*[3]

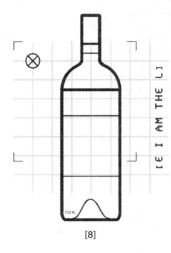

[8]

LIFE

Life and eternal life constitute a consistent theme of this book. Jesus promises eternal life to people who believe in him, the source of life. We miss the point if we think that Jesus is only promising a life that goes on and on endlessly. It is about being in a fulfilling relationship with God now and for ever. We enter that life *now*, and it continues on after death. It is quality life: life as it was meant to be. When we believe in Jesus, we pass from 'death' into this 'life'.

everyone born of the Spirit.'

9'How can this be?' Nicodemus asked.

10'You are Israel's teacher,' said Jesus, 'and do you not understand these things? 11I tell you the truth, we speak of what we know, and we testify to what we have seen, but still you people do not accept our testimony. 12I have spoken to you of earthly things and you do not believe; how then will you believe if I speak of heavenly things? 13No-one has ever gone into heaven except the one who came from heaven – the Son of Man. 14Just as Moses lifted up the snake in the desert, so the Son of Man must be lifted up, 15that everyone who believes in him may have eternal life.

16'For God so loved the world that he gave his one and only Son, that whoever believes in him shall not perish but have eternal life. 17For God did not send his Son into the world to condemn the world, but to save the world through him. 18Those who believe in him are not condemned, but those who do not believe stand condemned already because they have not believed in the name of God's one and only Son. 19This is the verdict: Light has come into the world, but people loved darkness instead of light because their deeds were evil. 20All those who do evil hate the light, and will not come into the light for fear that their deeds will be exposed. 21But those who live by the truth come into the light, so that it may be seen plainly that what they have done has been done through God.'

John the Baptist's testimony about Jesus

22After this, Jesus and his disciples went out into the Judean countryside, where he spent some time with them, and baptised. 23Now John also was baptising at Aenon near Salim, because there was plenty of water, and people were constantly coming to be baptised. 24(This was before John was put in prison.) 25An argument developed between some of John's disciples and a certain Jew over the matter of

Confusing, or what? What is reality? Where is reality? How can I get a grip on it? And even if I take the line that 'reality' doesn't need to exist in the way that some describe it, I have to recognize that in saying it, I have in fact constructed another 'reality' in which that comment makes sense.

Speculation

The second reaction I get is the one that usually starts with the words: 'When I think about "god", I like to think of him or her as ...' Then what I usually hear is a description of a 'being' who amazingly appears to fit the projected ideals – or mirror image – of the person speaking. Martin Wroe, writing in the Observer a few years back, describes this kind of 'image-projection':

> Religion has been reduced to the level of just one of more consumer choice. Ours is the age of the DIY god, where you make your deity to fit your lifestyle ... It would have parallels with the idol worship of ancient cultures were it not for the fact that the worshipper always remains firmly in control of the deity, adapting it at the slightest hint that it might interfere inconveniently with his or her lifestyle.[4]

Two reactions: two outcomes. The first one potentially leads to despair (will this 'god' ever reveal himself?), while the second nearly always leads to some form of speculation (the 'god' I'm happiest with is ...).

But John lays aside both these approaches. He regards the first as unnecessary and the second as simply wishful thinking, for he claims to have found in the person of Jesus Christ the answer to every person's quest for 'truth' and 'reality'.

'In the beginning was the *Word*.' Words of course are vital. They put us in touch. When

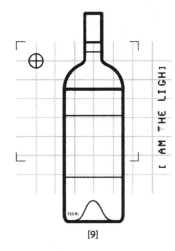

[9]

THE FATHER

Jesus commonly refers to God as his 'Father'. Jesus is unique among leaders of world religions in his claim that he can bring people into an intimate relationship with God. They also can know him as 'Father', with all its connotations of closeness, care and loving discipline. Jesus has no hesitation in making two other claims. First, his words and actions reveal to us what 'the Father' is like. Secondly, and even more astonishingly, he has identity with the 'Father'. Whoever has seen him has seen the Father.

ceremonial washing. [26]They came to John and said to him, 'Rabbi, that man who was with you on the other side of the Jordan — the one you testified about — well, he is baptising, and everyone is going to him.'

[27] To this John replied, 'A person can receive only what is given from heaven. [28]You yourselves can testify that I said, "I am not the Christ but am sent ahead of him." [29]The bride belongs to the bridegroom. The friend who attends the bridegroom waits and listens for him, and is full of joy when he hears the bridegroom's voice. That joy is mine, and it is now complete. [30]He must become greater; I must become less.

[31]'The one who comes from above is above all; the one who is from the earth belongs to the earth, and speaks as one from the earth. The one who comes from heaven is above all. [32]He testifies to what he has seen and heard, but no-one accepts his testimony. [33]The person who has accepted it has certified that God is truthful. [34]For the one whom God has sent speaks the words of God, for God gives the Spirit without limit. [35]The Father loves the Son and has placed everything in his hands. [36]Those who believe in the Son have eternal life, but those who reject the Son will not see life, for God's wrath remains on them.'

you are waiting for a 'word' from someone it conjures up a picture of suspense and expectation. When you do not hear a 'word' it implies loss of communication and distance, and an ignorance which detracts from life. There's that great moment in *Apollo 13* when the space capsule re-enters the Earth's atmosphere and communication goes dead. The engineers and flight control staff at NASA are left worrying that the problems experienced earlier in the flight will finally destroy the craft and its astronauts. Then there are the families. After a silence that seems endless there is a crackle over the speakers and the words, 'Houston, we have contact ...'

Here in John's opening words we have a 'Word' that lives with God, that is God and that has been with God from the very beginning of time. What then is this 'Word'? John quite literally 'fleshes it out' a few lines further on. For in verse 14 it becomes clear that this 'Word' by which God speaks and acts is none other than the hero of John's story, Jesus Christ. He is God's eternal and powerful 'Word', who actively communicates what we need to know about who God is, what his purposes are, and how he is to bring them about in the world at large, and in the lives of individuals and communities.

This is an extraordinary opening to any book. What if God does speak, and you could know about him and find out what he is like? But more than this: what if you could encounter him, be 'put in touch' with him, so to speak – communicate with him, know him? Extraordinary though it is, this is precisely what John is telling us in the first lines of his Gospel.

Perhaps you've never listened to this particular 'Word' before, or allowed it to address you. As with all words, you are free to ignore it. In fact, John says that this has been a common response down the years. Changing the metaphor to 'light', he says that 'The true light that gives light to everyone was coming into the world. He was in the world, and

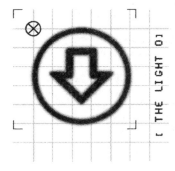

[THE LIGHT 01]

[10]

SAMARITANS

The Samaritans lived largely in the central area of Israel between Galilee in the north and Judea to the south. The bitterness felt between the Samaritan and Jewish peoples resulted from a perception that the Samaritans were a splinter group within Judaism, having an alternative centre for worshipping God. Jesus ignores the traditional barriers and speaks to the woman. There may be a direct contrast with the story about Nicodemus in chapter 3. The morally impeccable, religious man needs Jesus Christ, as does the immoral, unorthodox woman.

CHAPTER [4]

Jesus talks with a Samaritan woman

¹The Pharisees heard that Jesus was gaining and baptising more disciples than John, ²although in fact it was not Jesus who baptised, but his disciples. ³When the Lord learned of this, he left Judea and went back once more to Galilee.

⁴Now he had to go through Samaria. ⁵So he came to a town in Samaria called Sychar, near the plot of ground Jacob had given to his son Joseph. ⁶Jacob's well was there, and Jesus, tired as he was from the journey, sat down by the well. It was about the sixth hour.

⁷When a Samaritan woman came to draw water, Jesus said to her, 'Will you give me a drink?' ⁸(His disciples had gone into the town to buy food.)

⁹The Samaritan woman said to him, 'You are a Jew and I am a Samaritan woman. How can you ask me for a drink?' (For Jews do not associate with Samaritans.)

¹⁰Jesus answered her, 'If you knew the gift of God and who it is that asks you for

though the world was made through him, the world did not recognise him. He came to that which was his own, but his own did not receive him' (1:9–11).

But the Word continues to speak, even though it meets with rejection and refusal. Perhaps we ought now to listen. What then does Jesus, God's 'living Word', communicate?

The answer to the question of 'God'

The first thing John draws attention to is the fact that in the person of Jesus, God communicates the answer to the quest for himself. John puts it this way: 'No-one has ever seen God, but God the One and Only, who is at the Father's side, has made him known' (1:18). The Greek word translated here as 'the One and Only' is *monogēnes*, which means 'the only one of its kind or class'. If you are looking for God, then in the person of Jesus you will find him, says John. He came *from* God, and *was* God (1:1).

This identification that Jesus makes between himself and 'the one true God' (as the Jews put it) arises again and again in the pages of John. In 5:17 18, for example, he says, 'My Father is always at his work to this very day, and I, too, am working.' 'For this reason', records John, 'the Jews tried all the harder to kill him; not only was he breaking the Sabbath, but he was even calling God his own Father, making himself equal with God.' Or take chapter 14, where one of his friends asks Jesus to show them God the Father, for then they will be satisfied. 'Don't you know me, Philip, even after I have been among you such a long time?' replies Jesus. 'Anyone who has seen me has seen the Father' (14:8–9). Or take the opposition he encounters in chapter 10. It arises primarily because Jesus is claiming equal status with God himself. 'I and the Father are one', he says. When the Jews then try to stone him, he asks, 'I have shown you many great miracles from the Father. For which of these do you stone me?' They reply, 'We are not stoning you for any of these … but for

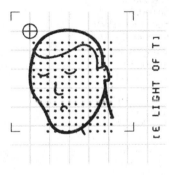

[11]

MESSIAH

At this time the imminent arrival of a special messenger from God was popularly expected. The historic writings of the Jewish people promised a coming 'Messiah' (the Hebrew word) or 'Christ' (the same word in Greek). Both mean 'the anointed one' – the one specially commissioned by God for his work. Some expected this Messiah to be a political-military deliverer who would bring an end to the Roman occupation of Palestine. Others looked for him to lead a revival of genuine worship among the Jewish people. Jesus challenged these popular expectations.

a drink, you would have asked him and he would have given you living water.'

¹¹'Sir,' the woman said, 'you have nothing to draw with and the well is deep. Where can you get this living water? ¹²Are you greater than our father Jacob, who gave us the well and drank from it himself, as did also his sons and his flocks and herds?'

¹³Jesus answered, 'All who drink this water will be thirsty again, ¹⁴but those who drink the water I give them will never thirst. Indeed, the water I give them will become in them a spring of water welling up to eternal life.'

¹⁵The woman said to him, 'Sir, give me this water so that I won't get thirsty and have to keep coming here to draw water.'

¹⁶He told her, 'Go, call your husband and come back.'

¹⁷'I have no husband,' she replied.

Jesus said to her, 'You are right when you say you have no husband. ¹⁸The fact is, you have had five husbands, and the man you now have is not your husband. What you

have just said is quite true.'

¹⁹'Sir,' the woman said, 'I can see that you are a prophet. ²⁰Our ancestors worshipped on this mountain, but you Jews claim that the place where we must worship is in Jerusalem.'

²¹Jesus declared, 'Believe me, woman, a time is coming when you will worship the Father neither on this mountain nor in Jerusalem. ²²You Samaritans worship what you do not know; we worship what we do know, for salvation is from the Jews. ²³Yet a time is coming and has now come when the true worshippers will worship the Father in spirit and truth, for they are the kind of worshippers the Father seeks. ²⁴God is spirit, and his worshippers must worship in spirit and in truth.'

²⁵The woman said, 'I know that Messiah' (called Christ) 'is coming. When he comes, he will explain everything to us.'

²⁶Then Jesus declared, 'I who speak to you am he.'

blasphemy, because you, a mere human being, claim to be God' (10:30–33).

That Jesus claims equality or identity with God is clear-cut in John. And of course it led to an explosion of scandal among his contemporaries, many of whom would have recited both morning and evening the Jewish prayer recorded in Deuteronomy 6:4:'Hear, O Israel: The Lord our God, the Lord is one.' They didn't miss the fact that what Jesus claims, and what John records, is that this living God, the creator of the universe, who has existed and will exist eternally, was personally present in Jesus in such a way that the only terminology in which you could adequately describe him was as God himself. It was such a claim that ultimately led to his death. But the claim lives on. You cannot read John's Gospel without being confronting by it time and time again.

This was one of the things that eventually convinced the Oxford don, C. S. Lewis, to believe in Jesus Christ and become a Christian. He later wrote to his friend Arthur Greeves: 'The doctrine of Christ's divinity seems to me not something stuck on which you can unstick but something that peeps out at every point so that you'd have to unravel the whole web to get rid of it.'[5]

The claim that Lewis accepts here is of course an enormous one. He arrived at it by studying the New Testament Gospels and being persuaded by the evidence that he found there. Of course, I do not expect to convince you of it immediately. It may be that you have never before seriously entertained the possibility that Jesus was God. But I do want to persuade you to immerse yourself in the pages of John's Gospel because it claims to answer the big quest. Like Lewis, you may be in for some surprises. I can do no more than this, and you should be satisfied with no less. For if the answer to the question of 'God' is settled, then all other questions can be framed in their proper context and the meaning of life can be unlocked.

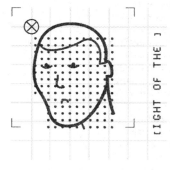

[LIGHT OF THE]

[12]

BELIEF

'Belief' dominates John's book from the beginning and is much more than giving mental assent. John's emphasis reminds us that he does not write in the style of a journalist seeking simply to inform. Belief is what he is after. Belief includes assenting to objective facts but moves beyond this to commitment. John unfolds a range of responses to Jesus, including a refusal to believe by those people apparently most likely to respond with enthusiasm.

The disciples rejoin Jesus

27Just then his disciples returned and were surprised to find him talking with a woman. But no-one asked, 'What do you want?' or 'Why are you talking with her?'

28Then, leaving her water jar, the woman went back to the town and said to the people, 29'Come, see a man who told me everything I ever did. Could this be the Christ?' 30They came out of the town and made their way towards him.

31Meanwhile his disciples urged him, 'Rabbi, eat something.'

32But he said to them, 'I have food to eat that you know nothing about.'

33Then his disciples said to each other, 'Could someone have brought him food?'

34'My food,' said Jesus, 'is to do the will of him who sent me and to finish his work. 35Do you not say, "Four months more and then the harvest"? I tell you, open your eyes and look at the fields! They are ripe for harvest. 36Even now those who reap draw their wages, even now they harvest the crop for eternal life, so that the sower and the reaper may be glad together. 37Thus the saying "One sows and another reaps" is true. 38I sent you to reap what you have not worked for. Others have done the hard work, and you have reaped the benefits of their labour.'

Many Samaritans believe

39Many of the Samaritans from that town believed in him because of the woman's testimony, 'He told me everything I ever did.' 40So when the Samaritans came to him, they urged him to stay with them, and he stayed two days. 41And because of his words many more became believers.

42They said to the woman, 'We no longer believe just because of what you said; now we have heard for ourselves, and we know that this man really is the Saviour of the world.'

Jesus heals the official's son

43After the two days he left for Galilee.

Here is the point to start at if you are thinking about Christianity. It will take you straight to the heart of the matter and focus your mind in the right place. Many understand Christianity as another religious 'system' or – worse still – as a series of regulations or principles that have to be followed. It is primarily neither of these things. As the German Christian martyr Dietrich Bonhoeffer put it, 'Christ is not the bringer of a new religion, but the bringer of God.'[6]

The answer to the question of 'humanity'

But John goes on from here. For alongside Jesus' uniquely divine status, he also stresses that Jesus was fully *human*. He says, 'The Word became flesh and made his dwelling among us' (1:14). Today we may not think this worth recording. We assume that Jesus was human: the problem for us is his divinity. But John probably emphasizes the point because in his day there were some – known technically as 'docetists' – who argued that Jesus was truly divine but only 'seemed' or 'appeared' to be human.[7] John counters this view by using blunt language about Jesus' humanity. There are a number of words he could have used to describe this, but he chooses to use the most basic word for the human body: 'flesh' (*sarx*). To give some idea of the connotation of this word, it is often used by Paul in some of his New Testament letters to draw a contrast between the 'earthly' desires of men and women who do not live according to God's pattern and those who respond to the new impulses that God implants by his Spirit.[8] The former are said to live 'according to the sinful nature' (*sarx*). John is not suggesting here that Jesus' nature was sinful. In fact, later in the Gospel he records his challenge to the religious authorities: 'Can any of you prove me guilty of sin?' (8:46). They could not.

So John's point here is not that Jesus was made like us in *every* way: for we *do* sin. It was

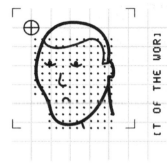

[13]

44(Now Jesus himself had pointed out that prophets have no honour in their own country.) 45When he arrived in Galilee, the Galileans welcomed him. They had seen all that he had done in Jerusalem at the Passover Feast, for they also had been there.

46Once more he visited Cana in Galilee, where he had turned the water into wine. And there was a certain royal official whose son lay sick at Capernaum. 47When this man heard that Jesus had arrived in Galilee from Judea, he went to him and begged him to come and heal his son, who was close to death.

48'Unless you people see miraculous signs and wonders,' Jesus told him, 'you will never believe.'

49The royal official said, 'Sir, come down before my child dies.'

50Jesus replied, 'You may go. Your son will live.'

The man took Jesus at his word and departed. 51While he was still on the way, his servants met him with the news that his boy was living. 52When he enquired as to the time when his son got better, they said to him, 'The fever left him yesterday at the seventh hour.'

53Then the father realised that this was the exact time at which Jesus had said to him, 'Your son will live.'

So he and all his household believed.

54This was the second miraculous sign that Jesus performed, having come from Judea to Galilee.

rather to make the point that Jesus was made in every way like us *apart from* sinning. As Martin Luther put it, Jesus 'ate, drank, slept, walked; was weary, sorrowful, rejoicing; he wept and he laughed; he knew hunger and thirst and sweat; he talked, he toiled, he prayed … so that there was no difference between him and other men, save only this – that he was God and had no sin.'

This 'demonstration' – if we can call it that – of what it means to be human is a demonstration of humanity as God intended it to be. We see a brief glimpse of this in Genesis 1 – 2, at the beginning of the Bible, before the catastrophic rebellion of human beings against God's word, which is recorded in Genesis 3. But Jesus never knew what it was to rebel against God.

So John's 'double whammy' here is that Jesus combines within himself both true divinity and true humanity. If you want to know what God is like, says John, look at Jesus Christ. If you want to know what it means to be truly human, look at Jesus Christ. He not only demonstrated fully, completely, and perfectly in his own life what it means to be truly human, but he became human precisely to enable us to live properly human lives. To quote the great reformer Martin Luther once more: 'God became man so that man might become fully human.'[9] We will explore this question in more detail in the next chapter. For clearly the claim being made here by John is as profound and contemporary as the one that Jesus is fully divine.

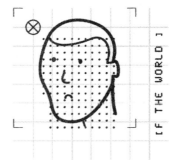

[14]

The answer to the quest for the knowledge of God
Douglas Coupland's book *After God*, which I quoted at the start of this chapter, closes with the following passage:

FESTIVALS

Jesus' visits to Jerusalem are linked in the story to major Jewish festivals (see also 2:13; 7:2; 10:22; 12:12). Each year people celebrated significant events in the life of the nation of Israel.

- Feast of Tabernacles: living in temporary shelters during the festival recalled God's guidance during the desert wanderings of their ancestors when, as refugees, they had fled from Egypt.

- Feast of Dedication: thanksgiving for the reinstatement of worship in the Jerusalem temple, after dominating Gentile rulers had desecrated the place with their idols.

- Passover: see note on 'The temple' (2:12-16).

CHAPTER [5]

The healing at the pool

[1]Some time later, Jesus went up to Jerusalem for a feast of the Jews. [2]Now there is in Jerusalem near the Sheep Gate a pool, which in Aramaic is called Bethesda and which is surrounded by five covered colonnades. [4]Here a great number of disabled people used to lie – the blind, the lame, the paralysed. [5]One who was there had been an invalid for thirty-eight years. [6]When Jesus saw him lying there and learned that he had been in this condition for a long time, he asked him, 'Do you want to get well?'

[7]'Sir,' the invalid replied, 'I have no-one to help me into the pool when the water is stirred. While I am trying to get in, someone else goes down ahead of me.'

[8]Then Jesus said to him, 'Get up! Pick up your mat and walk.' [9]At once the man was cured; he picked up his mat and walked.

The day on which this took place was a Sabbath, [10]and so the Jews said to the man who had been healed, 'It is the Sabbath; the law forbids you to carry your mat.'

Now – here is my secret: I tell it to you with an openness of heart that I doubt I shall ever achieve again, so I pray that you are in a quiet room as you hear these words. My secret is that I need God – that I am sick and can no longer make it alone. I need God to help me give, because I no longer seem to be capable of giving; to help me be kind, as I no longer seem capable of kindness; to help me love, as I seem beyond being able to love.[10]

What John offers us is precisely the answer to Coupland's quest. For in Jesus Christ, God's presence and help is granted and made available. But how does this happen? How is God's presence made known?

In the community of believers

John describes first of all the impact of this encounter upon those who responded to it. 'The word became flesh and made his dwelling among us. We have seen his glory' (1:14). 'From the fulness of his grace we have all received one blessing after another' (1:16). He speaks from within a community of believers who have opened their lives to the presence of God in Jesus Christ.

Perhaps you have noticed this among Christians around you. 'I can't quite put my finger on it,' you're thinking, 'but there does seem to be something different about them.' Perhaps they do seem to exhibit a consciousness of the presence of God which as yet is not part of your own experience.

In the lives of individuals

John puts it in a nutshell: 'He [Jesus] came to that which was his own, but his own did not receive him. Yet to all who received him, to those who believed in his name, he gave the

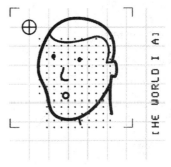

[THE WORLD I A]

[15]

[11]But he replied, 'The man who made me well said to me, "Pick up your mat and walk."'

[12]So they asked him,

'Who is this fellow who told you to pick it up and walk?'

[13]The man who was healed had no idea who it was, for Jesus had slipped away into the crowd that was there.

[14]Later Jesus found him at the temple and said to him, 'See, you are well again. Stop sinning or something worse may happen to you.' [15]The man went away and told the Jews that it was Jesus who had made him well.

right to become children of God – children born not of natural descent, nor of human decision or a husband's will, but born of God' (1:11–13).

John speaks here in terms of a new relationship with God in which believers are made his 'children'. They 'know' God in a new way and relate to him personally. Perhaps you've heard Christians talking in this way about their faith. They say things like, 'When I first came to know God personally …', or they describe themselves as having 'a personal relationship with Jesus'. What they are expressing by using these phrases is clearly something much more than knowing something *about* Jesus. There are many who know a great deal *about* Jesus, but who do not claim to know him in a personal way. No, this sort of language is altogether different from an abstract or intellectual knowledge. It is deeply personal and is characterized by the kind of words that you would use of other personal relationships. Jesus himself uses this language of his followers. In 10:14, for example, he uses the metaphor of a shepherd and his sheep. 'I am the good shepherd,' he says. 'I know my sheep and my sheep know me.' This implies an opening up on both sides of the relationship; a mutual understanding between Jesus and the individual.

This then is the goal of God's 'speaking' through his Son Jesus: that by receiving him and believing in him we too may become children of God, knowing him and being known by him, loving him and being loved by him, trusting him and living out his life among others.

God speaks

The Gospel of John that you have in your hands is therefore a 'word' from God. In it, by its focus upon Jesus Christ, God continues to speak about the greatest questions ever to face the human race:

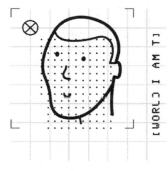

[16]

THE SABBATH

The Jewish people took Saturday as a day off work because they saw it as a divinely appointed rest day. It was not a free day. The Sabbath carried with it rules of behaviour to enhance relaxation and undistracted worship of God. Over the centuries, however, the rules governing the Sabbath grew tighter, defining more and more minutely what constituted work. Jesus gladly celebrated the Sabbath but refused to be bound by restrictive practices imposed by religious teachers. Caring for people in need must not be divorced from worship.

Life through the Son

16So, because Jesus was doing these things on the Sabbath, the Jews persecuted him. 17Jesus said to them, 'My Father is always at his work to this very day, and I, too, am working.' 18For this reason the Jews tried all the harder to kill him; not only was he breaking the Sabbath, but he was even calling God his own Father, making himself equal with God.

19Jesus gave them this answer: 'I tell you the truth, the Son can do nothing by himself; he can do only what he sees his Father doing, because whatever the Father does the Son also does. 20For the Father loves the Son and shows him all he does. Yes, to your amazement he will show him even greater things than these. 21For just as the Father raises the dead and gives them life, even so the Son gives life to whom he is pleased to give it. 22Moreover, the Father judges no-one, but has entrusted all judgment to the Son, 23that all may honour the Son just as they honour the Father. Whoever does not honour the Son does not honour the Father, who sent him.

24'I tell you the truth, those who hear my word and believe him who sent me have eternal life and will not be condemned; they have crossed over from death to life. 25I tell you the truth, a time is coming and has now come when the dead will hear the voice of the Son of God and those who hear will live. 26For as the Father has life in himself, so he has granted the Son to have life in himself. 27And he has given him authority to judge because he is the Son of Man.

28'Do not be amazed at this, for a time is coming when all who are in their graves will hear his voice 29and come out – those who have done good will rise to live, and those who have done evil will rise to be condemned. 30By myself I can do nothing; I judge only as I hear, and my judgment is just, for I seek not to please myself but him who sent me.

– who God is and how he can be known,
– who Jesus is and what he came to do,
– who we are and how we should live.

In the stories about him that follow, countless people have gone beyond the words on the page, and have 'encountered' this man, and by encountering him have been brought into a new perception of life, the universe and everything.

You are invited by John to do the same.

[R E A L   L I V E S]

DAVE MUNCK

Dave is a third-year theology student at Wycliffe Hall, Oxford.

My essential thoughts about God before I came to Oxford were that I was good enough for him if he existed, and if he didn't, it didn't matter. Either way, I was fine, so I didn't waste any time thinking about it. That was until I met a Christian who asked me if I was actually good enough for God. When I thought about it, it wasn't hard

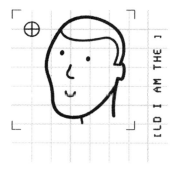

[17]

Testimonies about Jesus

[31]'If I testify about myself, my testimony is not valid. [32]There is another who testifies in my favour, and I know that his testimony about me is valid.

[33]'You have sent to John and he has testified to the truth. [34]Not that I accept human testimony; but I mention it that you may be saved. [35]John was a lamp that burned and gave light, and you chose for a time to enjoy his light.

[36]'I have testimony weightier than that of John. For the very work that the Father has given me to finish, and which I am doing, testifies that the Father has sent me. [37]And the Father who sent me has himself testified concerning me. You have never heard his voice nor seen his form, [38]nor does his word dwell in you, for you do not believe the one he sent. [39]You diligently study the Scriptures because you think that by them you possess eternal life. These are the Scriptures that testify about me, [40]yet you refuse to come to me to have life.

[41]'I do not accept human praise, [42]but I know you. I know that you do not have the love of God in your hearts. [43]I have come in my Father's name, and you do not accept me; but if others come in their own names, you will accept them. [44]How can you believe if you accept praise from one another, yet make no effort to obtain the praise that comes from the only God?

[45]'But do not think I will accuse you before the Father. Your accuser is Moses, on whom your hopes are set. [46]If you believed Moses, you would believe me, for he wrote about me. [47]But since you do not believe what he wrote, how are you going to believe what I say?'

to see that my self-opinion didn't reflect the reality of who I was, and if God existed, there was no way I matched up to his standards.

As a result, the issue of the existence of God took on a lot more significance, so I ended up spending a lot of time thinking about it. After a couple of weeks of deep thought, I was convinced that I had come to the right conclusion: God didn't exist, and I was an atheist. Everything that I understood of life, philosophy and God suggested that we created God because we couldn't deal with questions like 'Who am I?' and 'Why am I here?'

In the spring term of my first year, I went along to one of the talks at a university mission, which made little impression. Afterwards, I was introduced to one of the missioners, and ended up in a long conversation with him. He suggested that God had designed human beings to be in a relationship with him. This was something I hadn't considered, and by the end of our discussion, I found myself back where I had been the term before, wondering if God existed, knowing that if he did, it had a big significance for my life.

In the second half of term, there were some weekly discussion groups organized in a pub, and I went along to find out more. We discussed what the Bible teaches about Jesus Christ, and the significance he has for my life. I could see clearly that the Bible claimed that Jesus is

[18]

CHAPTER [6]

Jesus feeds the five thousand

¹Some time after this, Jesus crossed to the far shore of the Sea of Galilee (that is, the Sea of Tiberias), ²and a great crowd of people followed him because they saw the miraculous signs he had performed on the sick. ³Then Jesus went up on a mountainside and sat down with his disciples. ⁴The Jewish Passover Feast was near.

⁵When Jesus looked up and saw a great crowd coming towards him, he said to Philip, 'Where shall we buy bread for these people to eat?' ⁶He asked this only to test him, for he already had in mind what he was going to do.

⁷Philip answered him, 'Eight months' wages would not buy enough bread for each one to have a bite!'

⁸Another of his disciples, Andrew, Simon Peter's brother, spoke up, ⁹'Here is a boy with five small barley loaves and two small fish, but how far will they go among so many?'

God, and he came to earth to die in my place for the wrong I have done against God. The difficulty I had was accepting that the Bible was true, and that the Jesus who spoke in it was the Jesus of history. The big question was, 'Did Jesus rise from the dead?' If he didn't, then the Bible was more religious gibberish, but if he did ... ? As we looked at the evidence, I became convinced, despite my scientific prejudices, that the Jesus of the Bible was the Jesus of history, and that he did actually rise.

It took me a couple of weeks to think through the implications that resulted from Jesus being who he claimed to be. I couldn't just let it lie; I knew I had rebelled against God, and the only way of dealing with the problem was to believe and trust in Jesus' death on the cross.

I put my trust in Jesus nearly three years ago, and I would be lying if I said it had been easy. Lots of things haven't changed: I still have to shave, I still get backache, I still have to work, but my life as a whole has been transformed. Trying to follow Jesus is hard and has its clear ups and downs, but the truth doesn't change. I am now reading theology, and find that the more I understand the Bible, the more I am convinced that Jesus came to die for me, that he rose again, and putting my trust in him is the best thing I could ever do.

[19]

¹⁰Jesus said, 'Make the people sit down.'
There was plenty of grass in that place, and
they sat down, about five thousand of them.

¹¹Jesus then took the
loaves, gave thanks, and
distributed to those who
were seated as much as
they wanted. He did the
same with the fish.

[2] Who am I?

'That whole idea of questioning where you are and why you are is something I go through all the time.'
KEANU REEVES, *TIME OUT*, JUNE 1999

'Doth any here know me? ... Who is it that can tell me who I am?'
SHAKESPEARE, *KING LEAR* I. IV, SEVENTEENTH CENTURY AD

'Nothing then is more wretched anywhere than man of all that breathes and creeps upon the earth.'
HOMER, EIGHTH CENTURY BC

What does it mean to be human?

The question 'Who am I?' is one of the most basic questions a human being can ask, and it has been around since time began. It is also potentially a rather scary one. The sociologist Peter Berger has bluntly put it into historical focus for us: 'Society antedates us and it will survive us. It was there before we were born and it will be there after we are

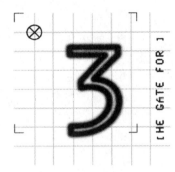

[20]

Moses was the first prophet to Israel, almost 2,000 years prior to Jesus Christ. Despite Moses' huge stature, generations of Jews awaited another prophet he had promised, greater than himself. A long line of prophets throughout Israel's history, speaking God's truth into the life of the nation, had not revealed this awaited prophet. With the arrival of Jesus Christ, speaking and acting with an extraordinary authority, this issue of the promised prophet came to the fore. John's Gospel wants us to connect this promise with Jesus' arrival.

[12]When they had all had enough to eat, he said to his disciples, 'Gather the pieces that are left over. Let nothing be wasted.' [13]So they gathered them and filled twelve baskets with the pieces of the five barley loaves left over by those who had eaten.

[14]After the people saw the miraculous sign that Jesus did, they began to say, 'Surely this is the Prophet who is to come into the world.' [15]Jesus, knowing that they intended to come and make him king by force, withdrew again to a mountain by himself.

Jesus walks on the water

[16]When evening came, his disciples went down to the lake, [17]where they got into a boat and set off across the lake for Capernaum. By now it was dark, and Jesus had not yet joined them. [18]A strong wind was blowing and the waters grew rough. [19]When they had rowed three or three and a half miles, they saw Jesus approaching the boat, walking on the water; and they were terrified. [20]But he said to them,

'It is I; don't be afraid.'

dead. Our lives are but episodes in its majestic march through time. In sum, society is the walls of our imprisonment in history.'[1]

Rather bleakly put, I grant you. But true nevertheless: and it raises the pressing question of where human beings fit into the greater scheme of things. It is certainly a question that we must try to get some sort of a grip on if we are to make ultimate sense of our lives.

But perhaps the whole question of identity has taken a particularly acute form in our postmodern generation. Madonna can famously invent and reinvent her image from one year to the next, so that the outsider is completely in the dark as to who she really is, or wants to be. Perhaps she is playing out the different fantasies of self-image for which she is famous, partly as a defence mechanism, or partly as a way of trying to stay in the spotlight. As she herself has said, 'I won't be happy until I'm as famous as God.'[2] Or perhaps she, like many others, is really unsure who she really is. Whatever the case, Madonna's image-projection of herself betrays in vivid colours a deeper sense of cultural unease with the whole question of self-identity. As Kenneth Gergen has written, 'Under postmodern conditions, persons exist in a state of continuous construction and reconstruction; it is a world where anything goes that can be negotiated. Each reality of self gives way to reflexive questioning, irony, and ultimately the playful probing of yet another reality. The center fails to hold.'[3]

Or take Zygmunt Bauman's vivid description of the pressure on our sense of self-identity in a fast-moving and changing world: 'It is all around, salient and tangible, all-too-protruding in the rapidly ageing and abruptly devalued skills, in human bonds entered until further notice, in jobs which can be taken away without any notice, and the ever new allures of the consumer feast, each promising untried kinds of happiness while

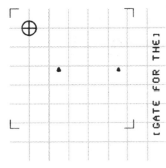

[GATE FOR THE]

[21]

Throughout the book we will encounter vivid sayings of Jesus about himself. These 'I am' sayings fall into two categories:
- concrete images (water, bread, shepherd, light)
- more abstract ideas (way, truth, life)

The sayings portray Jesus as the lasting answer to human quests – whether these are for satisfaction (bread, water), security and value (good shepherd), truth (light), or meaning (resurrection and life). Jesus draws a deliberate contrast between his promises and temporary remedies. You get thirsty again after drinking ordinary water, bread goes mouldy, and houses are burgled.

John 6:21–35

21Then they were willing to take him into the boat, and immediately the boat reached the shore where they were heading. 22The next day the crowd that had stayed on the opposite shore of the lake realised that only one boat had been there, and that Jesus had not entered it with his disciples, but that they had gone away alone. 23Then some boats from Tiberias landed near the place where the people had eaten the bread after the Lord had given thanks. 24Once the crowd realised that neither Jesus nor his disciples were there, they got into the boats and went to Capernaum in search of Jesus.

Jesus the bread of life

25When they found him on the other side of the lake, they asked him, 'Rabbi, when did you get here?'

26Jesus answered, 'I tell you the truth, you are looking for me, not because you saw miraculous signs but because you ate the loaves and had your fill. 27Do not work for food that spoils, but for food that endures to eternal life, which the Son of Man will give you. On him God the Father has placed his seal of approval.'

28Then they asked him, 'What must we do to do the works God requires?'

29Jesus answered, 'The work of God is this: to believe in the one he has sent.'

30So they asked him, 'What miraculous sign then will you give that we may see it and believe you? What will you do? 31Our ancestors ate the manna in the desert; as it is written: "He gave them bread from heaven to eat."'

32Jesus said to them, 'I tell you the truth, it is not Moses who has given you the bread from heaven, but it is my Father who gives you the true bread from heaven. 33For the bread of God is he who comes down from heaven and gives life to the world.'

34'Sir,' they said, 'from now on give us this bread.'

35Then Jesus declared, 'I am the bread of life. Whoever comes to me will never go

wiping the shine off the tried ones.'⁴

Oxford, exams, career, pay off student loan … The pressure is on. But will the life that I am being catapulted into help me to find out who I am? Will it give me the space to explore the question of who I was made to be? Will society ever progress to become a place where individuals are genuinely valued for who they are? More pertinently, will people like Madonna (and me?) ever really find out the answer to the age-long question, 'What does it mean to be the person I am?'

Jesus and the question of human identity

As you will recall, my aim in writing these chapters is to get you to read John's Gospel because it claims to offer answers to the most profound issues of human life: not least the question of who I am meant to be. It does so by describing the most radical human being that ever lived: Jesus Christ.

Take chapter 4, for example. Here we find Jesus with his disciples on his way back to his home patch of Galilee after talking with the Jewish leader Nicodemus in Jerusalem (recorded in 3:1–15). The most direct route back to Galilee led through the area of Samaria (now the West Bank region), and the story picks up where Jesus stops at midday near the city of Sychar (near present-day Nablus). The disciples had gone into town to get some food, and Jesus sits by the well. Along comes a woman, and Jesus talks with her.

This at least is the bare outline of the story. But even this much shows that Jesus is radical in his social attitudes. For this woman's 'identity' would have been enough to cause any right-minded Jew of the time – let alone a rabbi – to turn on his heals and leave without further notice. But Jesus transcends sexual, cultural, national and religious barriers even to engage her in conversation.

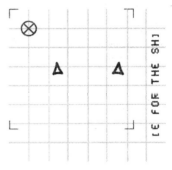

[22]

BREAD FROM HEAVEN

The memory of their deliverance from slavery in Egypt gripped Jesus' contemporaries. A forty-year period of wandering in the desert of the Sinai peninsula had followed. As travellers in such a barren environment, they were dependent for their food supply on divine intervention. They were miraculously provided with manna, a bread-like food, from the sky ('manna' is the Hebrew expression 'What is it?', their first question on seeing it). Jesus links into this image by claiming that he too is food from heaven, coming from God to give life.

hungry, and whoever believes in me will never be thirsty. 36But as I told you, you have seen me and still you do not believe. 37All that the Father gives me will come to me, and whoever comes to me I will never drive away. 38For I have come down from heaven not to do my will but to do the will of him who sent me. 39And this is the will of him who sent me, that I shall lose none of all that he has given me, but raise them up at the last day. 40For my Father's will is that all those who look to the Son and believe in him shall have eternal life, and I will raise them up at the last day.'

41At this the Jews began to grumble about him because he said, 'I am the bread that came down from heaven.' 42They said, 'Is this not Jesus, the son of Joseph, whose father and mother we know? How can he now say, "I came down from heaven"?'

43'Stop grumbling among yourselves,' Jesus answered. 44'No-one can come to me unless the Father who sent me draws them, and I will raise them up at the last day. 45It is written in the Prophets: "They will all be taught by God." Everyone who listens to the Father and learns from him comes to me. 46No-one has seen the Father except the one who is from God; only he has seen the Father. 47I tell you the truth, whoever believes has everlasting life. 48I am the bread of life. 49Your ancestors ate the manna in the desert, yet they died. 50But here is the bread that comes down from heaven, which people may eat and not die. 51I am the living bread that came down from heaven. Whoever eats of this bread will live for ever. This bread is my flesh, which I will give for the life of the world.'

52Then the Jews began to argue sharply among themselves, 'How can this man give us his flesh to eat?'

53Jesus said to them, 'I tell you the truth, unless you eat the flesh of the Son of Man and drink his blood, you have no life in you. 54Those who eat my flesh and drink my blood have eternal life, and I will raise them up at the last day. 55For my flesh is real food

First, she was a woman. The sex discrimination thing was around then too. Good-minded Jewish men didn't address women in public (even their wives) if they could avoid it. One group of first-century Pharisees was actually nicknamed 'the bruised and bleeding ones'. Because of the lengths to which they went to avert their gaze when a woman passed by, they were in the habit of walking into things like walls!

Secondly, she was a Samaritan. That is to say, she was a member of an ethnic minority group that the Jews considered at best to be half-caste because of their intermarriage with non-Jews several centuries before. So John's editorial statement in the second half of verse 9 ('Jews do not associate with Samaritans') is an understatement of enormous proportions. Most religious Jews would have skirted around Samaria altogether if they had to go from Jerusalem to Galilee. To have drunk from the same cup as a Samaritan woman, therefore, would have rendered Jesus ceremonially unclean in the eyes of the Jewish law.

Thirdly, as becomes clear later in the conversation, this woman is morally lax. Her sex life is all over the place. She has had five husbands already and is presently cohabiting with her boyfriend. All this is enough to evoke the severest scorn and condemnation from any self-respecting religious teacher. But not Jesus. He is well aware of the kind of person this woman is, and yet he goes out of his way to speak with her and help her.

It is difficult for us today to imagine the scandal that Jesus' actions here would have evoked. Like a person going out of his way to help another on the other side of an ethnic divide. Like a Serb standing up for the rights of a Kosovar Albanian. Like an Orangeman meeting the needs of a Catholic neighbour. But it feels right, doesn't it? If only we could get over these cultural and ethnic divisions, wouldn't the world be a better place? Of course, when you consider that this is God's very self in human form doing these things,

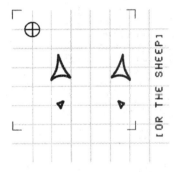

[23]

and my blood is real drink. 56Those who eat my flesh and drink my blood remain in me, and I in them. 57Just as the living Father sent me and I live because of the Father, so the one who feeds on me will live because of me. 58This is the bread that came down from heaven. Your ancestors ate manna and died, but whoever feeds on this bread will live for ever.' 59He said this while teaching in the synagogue in Capernaum.

Many disciples desert Jesus

60On hearing it, many of his disciples said, 'This is a hard teaching. Who can accept it?'

61Aware that his disciples were grumbling about this, Jesus said to them, 'Does this offend you? 62What if you see the Son of Man ascend to where he was before! 63The Spirit gives life; the flesh counts for nothing. The words I have spoken to you are spirit and they are life. 64Yet there are some of you who do not believe.' For Jesus had known from the beginning which of them did not believe and who would betray him. 65He

went on to say, 'This is why I told you that no-one can come to me unless the Father has enabled them.'

66From this time many of his disciples turned back and no longer followed him.

67'You do not want to leave too, do you?' Jesus asked the Twelve.

68Simon Peter answered him, 'Lord, to whom shall we go? You have the words of eternal life. 69We believe and know that you are the Holy One of God.'

70Then Jesus replied, 'Have I not chosen you, the Twelve? Yet one of you is a devil!' 71(He meant Judas, the son of Simon Iscariot, who, though one of the Twelve, was later to betray him.)

then the 'scandal' to contemporaries is magnified a thousand times. But so is the sense of 'rightness'. At last here is a true human being, treating others – whoever they are, whether a high-caste religious teacher like Nicodemus, or a low-caste woman like this one – without prejudice or bigotry.

The woman's self-perception

We can only guess at her own sense of self-identity. Perhaps her perception of herself reflected her social marginalization. She certainly expresses surprise ('You are a Jew and I am a Samaritan woman') when Jesus first asks her for a drink, suggesting that she was well aware of her social standing in the eyes of this foreigner (4:9). Perhaps, at a more mundane and human level, she also resented the daily trip in the heat of the day to collect water for herself and her 'family'. The drab monotony of the daily routine. She certainly jumps at the idea that this might be the last visit she has to make to the well in the heat of the day when Jesus later says that what he is offering her is a very different kind of water supply (4:15).

Whatever her self-perception, John is at pains to point out in this story that Jesus goes out of his way to meet her and to transform her situation. He is as concerned for her as he is for Nicodemus in the previous chapter – the VIP Jew. And, as the story develops, it becomes clear that as far as the question of 'what it means to be me' is concerned, Jesus radically reorientates this age-old question and shows that the answer to it does not depend primarily upon relationships with other people or with material possessions, but rather with himself. If we are to find the answer to the question 'Who am I?'; if we are to find 'satisfaction' in life, then – says Jesus – he is the person to whom we must relate.

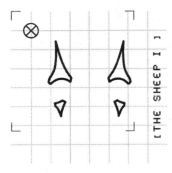

[24]

JESUS' SECRECY

Strangely enough, Jesus does not draw immediate attention to his miracles. He rejects the power of publicity. Why does he not make the most of his PR opportunity? Probably because sensationalism, drawing a crowd only interested in the miraculous, is not his intention. He demands understanding. He looks for people to go beyond the outward and to grasp the truth behind the miracles. Thinking clearly is not done best in a hyped-up atmosphere of emotional excitement. He shuns the manipulation of people.

CHAPTER [7]

Jesus goes to the Feast of Tabernacles

[1]After this, Jesus went around in Galilee, purposely staying away from Judea because the Jews there were waiting to take his life. [2]But when the Jewish Feast of Tabernacles was near, [3]Jesus' brothers said to him, 'You ought to leave here and go to Judea, so that your disciples may see the miracles you do. [4]No-one who wants to become a public figure acts in secret. Since you are doing these things, show yourself to the world.' [5]For even his own brothers did not believe in him.

[6]Therefore Jesus told them, 'The right time for me has not yet come; for you any time is right. [7]The world cannot hate you, but it hates me because I testify that what it does is evil. [8]You go to the Feast. I am not yet going up to this Feast, because for me the right time has not yet come.' [9]Having said this, he stayed in Galilee.

[10]However, after his brothers had left for the Feast, he went also, not publicly, but in secret. [11]Now at the Feast the Jews were

What it means to be human

This radical perspective is announced by Jesus early on in the conversation. But the woman is misled by the words that Jesus uses and quickly jumps to the wrong conclusion.

For after Jesus has asked her for a drink, and she has expressed her surprise, Jesus takes the conversation on to a different level altogether. 'If you knew the gift of God and who it is that asks you for a drink', he says, 'you would have asked him and he would have given you living water' (4:10). She is – perhaps understandably – confused by this statement and takes Jesus to be referring to 'moving' water: that is, the kind you'd get in a stream or river rather than a well. So she replies quite logically that as the well that Jesus is asking her to draw from is the only source of any kind of water for miles around, where is Jesus proposing to get hold of this 'moving' water?

But Jesus persists and invites her to take this picture of 'living' water as a metaphor for something much deeper. 'All who drink this water will be thirsty again', he says, 'but those who drink the water I give them will never thirst. Indeed, the water I give them will become in them a spring of water welling up to eternal life' (4:13–14).

At this point in the conversation misunderstanding rules big time. The woman is unable to hear what he is trying to communicate. She thinks he is talking about the satisfaction of *material* thirst, while Jesus is talking about the satisfaction of *spiritual* thirst. And the reason she cannot grasp this – says Jesus – is that she doesn't yet realize who it is that she is talking to.

If she had, she might have started to grasp the enormity of what Jesus is offering with this 'living' water. And by understanding this, she would have begun to latch on to the answer Jesus is offering her to the eternal question of what it means to be human. For what Jesus refers to here by this 'living water' is nothing less than the very life of God let

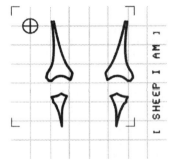

[25]

watching for Jesus and asking, 'Where is he?'

12Among the crowds there was widespread whispering about him. Some said, 'He is a good man.'

Others replied, 'No, he deceives the people.' 13But no-one would say anything publicly about him for fear of the Jews.

Jesus teaches at the Feast

14Not until halfway through the Feast did Jesus go up to the temple courts and begin to teach. 15The Jews were amazed and asked, 'How did this man get such learning without having studied?'

16Jesus answered, 'My teaching is not my own. It comes from him who sent me. 17Anyone who chooses to do the will of God will find out whether my teaching comes from God or whether I speak on my own. 18Those who speak on their own do so to gain honour for themselves, but he who works for the honour of the one who sent him is a man of truth; there is nothing false

about him. 19Has not Moses given you the law? Yet not one of you keeps the law. Why are you trying to kill me?'

20'You are demon-possessed,' the crowd answered. 'Who is trying to kill you?'

21Jesus said to them, 'I did one miracle, and you are all astonished. 22Yet, because Moses gave you circumcision (though actually it did not come from Moses, but from the patriarchs), you circumcise a child on the Sabbath. 23Now if a child can be circumcised on the Sabbath so that the law of Moses may not be broken, why are you angry with me for healing the whole person on the Sabbath? 24Stop judging by mere appearances, and make a right judgment.'

Is Jesus the Christ?

25At that point some of the people of Jerusalem began to ask, 'Isn't this the man they are trying to kill? 26Here he is, speaking publicly, and they are not saying a word to him. Have the authorities really concluded that he is the Christ? 27But we know where

loose like an 'eternal spring' of water in the lives of those who respond in faith to Jesus Christ. Later, Jesus speaks in more detail about this: 'Let anyone who is thirsty come to me and drink', he says. 'Whoever believes in me, as the Scripture has said, will have streams of living water flowing from within.' John then explains to the reader: 'By this he meant the Spirit, whom those who believed in him were later to receive' (7:37–39).

So the 'living water' Jesus is talking about is nothing less than God's very own personal presence, made available at the centre of our lives and experience both to 'refresh' us and to 'quench' our spiritual thirst.

Moreover, this 'personal presence' of God in the life of the individual is the key to the question of human identity that Jesus identifies for the woman, and therefore to the questions that we have been considering in this chapter. For we were not designed to exist in some spiritual void, seeking our identity and purpose simply at the level of the 'material'. Though there are many people who attempt to do just this, it will always result in a one-dimensional life. For if being truly human means understanding that we were made to know God, and in that relationship to find out who we truly are, then to deny this can only result in our having sub-human ideas about ourselves. 'Meaning' and 'identity' come – says Jesus – as we understand who made us. Or as the great fourth-century theologian Augustine famously put it as he spoke to God in prayer: 'you made us for yourself and our hearts find no peace until they rest in you'.[5]

Material beings living in a material world?

The woman, however, is unable to make the vital connection at this point, but sits happy with what she thinks (and certainly hopes) Jesus might be referring to. Jettisoning the 'spiritual' angle, she plumps for the material. 'Sir, give me this water so that I won't get

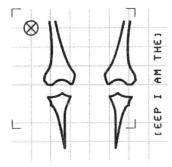

[26]

THE PHARISEES

The Pharisees were a religious group renowned for their purity and diligence in religious duty. It is perhaps surprising then that the relationship between the Pharisees and Jesus was one of confrontation. The opposition to Jesus which surfaces in the Gospel usually centres around the Pharisees. And Jesus' severest criticism is reserved for these people. Despite their rigorous beliefs, Jesus condemns them as viewing him on a purely human level. They generally failed to perceive Jesus as the fulfilment of their desires, and therefore rejected him and his claims.

this man is from; when the Christ comes, no-one will know where he is from.'

28Then Jesus, still teaching in the temple courts, cried out, 'Yes, you know me, and you know where I am from. I am not here on my own, but he who sent me is true. You do not know him, 29but I know him because I am from him and he sent me.'

30At this they tried to seize him, but no-one laid a hand on him, because his time had not yet come. 31Still, many in the crowd put their faith in him. They said, 'When the Christ comes, will he do more miraculous signs than this man?'

32The Pharisees heard the crowd whispering such things about him. Then the chief priests and the Pharisees sent temple guards to arrest him.

33Jesus said, 'I am with you for only a short time, and then I go to the one who sent me. 34You will look for me, but you will not find me; and where I am, you cannot come.'

35The Jews said to one another, 'Where does this man intend to go that we cannot find him? Will he go where our people live scattered among the Greeks, and teach the Greeks? 36What did he mean when he said, "You will look for me, but you will not find me," and "Where I am, you cannot come"?'

37On the last and greatest day of the Feast, Jesus stood and said in a loud voice, 'Let anyone who is thirsty come to me and drink. 38Whoever believes in me, as the Scripture has said, will have streams of living water flowing from within.' 39By this he meant the Spirit, whom those who believed in him were later to receive. Up to that time the Spirit had not been given, since Jesus had not yet been glorified.

40On hearing his words, some of the people said, 'Surely this man is the Prophet.'

41Others said, 'He is the Christ.'

Still others asked, 'How can the Christ come from Galilee? 42Does not the Scripture say that the Christ will come from David's family and from Bethlehem, the town where David lived?' 43Thus the people were

thirsty and have to keep coming here to draw water' (4:15). This is the ultimate water-privatization pay-off, an eternal water tap in her kitchen that never dries up!

Interesting, isn't it? In our discussion about 'identity', our contemporary culture gets very little beyond this woman's focus and dilemma. If only we could satisfy our material needs – so the argument goes – the question of human identity would be solved. If only I could … If only I had … As soon as I can afford to … Then …

But will it? If we were merely material beings, then to quench our thirst for material things would indeed provide satisfaction for the deepest longings of the human heart. But are we purely material beings? This is the question that Jesus probes throughout John's Gospel by his very presence. Certainly, those who do achieve wealth and fame do not often appear to be any happier than those who do not. In fact, wealth tends to bring its own problems gift-wrapped. Raquel Welch's words are worth pondering when she wrote at the height of her career:

> *I had acquired everything I wanted, yet I was totally miserable … I thought it was very peculiar that I had acquired everything I had wanted as a child – wealth, fame and accomplishment in my career. I had beautiful children, and a lifestyle that seemed terrific, yet I was totally and miserably unhappy. I found it very frightening that one could acquire all these things and still be so miserable.*

The obnoxious and unpalatable truth about wealth and status is that they nearly always fail to satisfy. They always crave for more.

But what Jesus offers the woman here is something far more fundamental, and his diagnosis of the human condition is equally more radical. In order to get her to the crucial point of recognition, he is uncannily direct. 'Go, call your husband and come back', he says

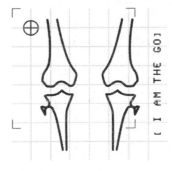

[27]

divided because of Jesus. ⁴⁴Some wanted to seize him, but no-one laid a hand on him.

[The earliest and most reliable manuscripts and other ancient witnesses do not have John 7:53 – 8:11.]

Unbelief of the Jewish leaders

⁴⁵Finally the temple guards went back to the chief priests and Pharisees, who asked them, 'Why didn't you bring him in?'

⁴⁶'No-one ever spoke the way this man does,' the guards declared.

⁴⁷'You mean he has deceived you also?' the Pharisees retorted. ⁴⁸'Has any of the rulers or of the Pharisees believed in him? ⁴⁹No! But this mob that knows nothing of the law – there is a curse on them.'

⁵⁰Nicodemus, who had gone to Jesus earlier and who was one of their own number, asked, ⁵¹'Does our law condemn people without first hearing them to find out what they are doing?'

⁵²They replied, 'Are you from Galilee, too? Look into it, and you will find that a prophet does not come out of Galilee.'

⁵³Then they all went home.

(4:16). This is not an invitation by Jesus for him to join her in some sort of group therapy. She doesn't need to be helped to face the disappointment of an 'almost' win on the pools. It is, rather, his way of facing her with her own real dilemma. For the real problem with our human natures, he suggests, is not that we are in need of material satisfaction (as she naïvely supposes), but rather that we are morally flawed and, because of this, our relationship with God is impaired to the point at which we are separated from God. The woman cannot escape the recognition of her own failure in this department, and appears content to face it, especially now that it has been exposed by Jesus. And the resulting implications that this 'revelation' of her past life has for her view of Jesus immediately become apparent. 'Sir', she says, 'I can see you are a prophet' (4:19). And how! We might easily add an exclamation mark to the text at this point, because – along with the statement about Jews not relating to Samaritans in 4:9 – it represents the second gigantic understatement in the story.

The big insight

Where does this rapier insight leave her? She has been taken on a roller-coaster ride of promise and misunderstanding, of extraordinary revelation and yet now of crippling uncertainty. One senses that this is a watershed moment. She is up against the wall. Jesus has got straight through to the heart of the matter and has exposed her real problem. She knows that her past life would for ever exclude her from participation in the worship of the community. She would always be an outsider as far as God's people were concerned.

The seventeenth-century philosopher Blaise Pascal wrote: 'Certainly nothing jolts us more rudely than this doctrine, and yet, but for this mystery, the most incomprehensible of all, we remain incomprehensible to ourselves.'[6] The 'doctrine' that Pascal refers to here

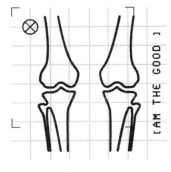

[28]

CHAPTER [8]

¹But Jesus went to the Mount of Olives. ²At dawn he appeared again in the temple courts, where all the people gathered round him, and he sat down to teach them. ³The teachers of the law and the Pharisees brought in a woman caught in adultery. They made her stand before the group ⁴and said to Jesus, 'Teacher, this woman was caught in the act of adultery. ⁵In the Law Moses commanded us to stone such women. Now what do you say?' ⁶They were using this question as a trap, in order to have a basis for accusing him.

But Jesus bent down and started to write on the ground with his finger. ⁷When they kept on questioning him, he straightened up and said to them, 'Let anyone of you who is without sin be the first to throw a stone at her.' ⁸Again he stooped down and wrote on the ground.

⁹At this, those who heard began to go away one at a time, the older ones first, until only Jesus was left, with the woman still standing there. ¹⁰Jesus straightened up and

is the plain teaching of the Bible that we are naturally not what we were meant to be. We do not enjoy and experience God's life as was intended, for the simple reason that our hearts are set on other things. We naturally do like to define ourselves to the exclusion of God, and of Jesus Christ. Moreover, there is nothing that we can do to rectify the situation. What does it mean to be human? Just as for the woman, it will mean coming to terms with the fact that we are not what we should be. We need help. But more than this: we need forgiveness from the one whom we have so outrageously excluded from our lives. And until we reach this point, we shall always fail to come to terms with who we really are. Like the woman, we may be tempted to define ourselves in ways which skirt around this central and inescapable fact. Human nature being what it is, we are often extremely able at this. But we cannot ultimately escape the fact. We are what the Bible calls 'sinners'.

This then is the point that the woman has reached. She can no longer run from Jesus. She has been cornered by his penetrating and prophetic insight. She has to deal with the moral thing. But how? She realizes that her moral failures obliterate her standing under the Jewish law, and ultimately cut her off from God himself. So she raises the religious question. 'Our ancestors worshipped on this mountain,' she says, 'but you Jews claim that the place where we must worship is in Jerusalem' (4:20).

This may be a diversionary tactic. You know the sort of thing. Talk about the differences between this religion and that. Good tactic – as ever. More likely, however, she is facing up to the consequences of what Jesus knows about her. What he has brought into the open about her private life makes her unable to relate to God in any way, shape or form. So how can she go on trying to relate to him? 'I am a sinner before God,' she is thinking, 'I must therefore make an offering for my sin; I must take that offering to the house of God to put myself right with him. But where should I take it? Gerizim or Jerusalem? Where – in essence – do I find God?'

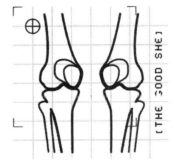

[THE GOOD SHE]

[29]

Light is employed as a powerful image of revelation throughout John's Gospel. Light is pictured as flooding the darkness, dispelling ignorance, and revealing truth. John focuses on Jesus as the one who brings light into the world, and is that light. The claim is that he brings some knowledge of God to everyone and, to those willing to see, he brings knowledge and life. Some choose to remain engulfed in darkness, unwilling to have their lives exposed to the truth. Jesus breaks through people's ignorance.

asked her, 'Woman, where are they? Has no-one condemned you?'

[11]'No-one, sir,' she said.

'Then neither do I condemn you,' Jesus declared. 'Go now and leave your life of sin.'

The validity of Jesus' testimony

[12]When Jesus spoke again to the people, he said, 'I am the light of the world. Whoever follows me will never walk in darkness, but will have the light of life.'

[13]The Pharisees challenged him, 'Here you are, appearing as your own witness; your testimony is not valid.'

[14]Jesus answered, 'Even if I testify on my own behalf, my testimony is valid, for I know where I came from and where I am going. But you have no idea where I come from or where I am going. [15]You judge by human standards; I pass judgment on no-one. [16]But if I do judge, my decisions are right, because I am not alone. I stand with the Father, who sent me. [17]In your own Law it is written that the testimony of two witnesses is valid. [18]I am one who testifies for myself; my other witness is the Father, who sent me.'

[19]Then they asked him, 'Where is your father?'

'You do not know me or my Father,' Jesus replied. 'If you knew me, you would know my Father also.' [20]He spoke these words while teaching in the temple area near the place where the offerings were put. Yet no-one seized him, because his time had not yet come.

[21]Once more Jesus said to them, 'I am going away, and you will look for me, and you will die in your sin. Where I go, you cannot come.'

[22]This made the Jews ask, 'Will he kill himself? Is that why he says, "Where I go, you cannot come"?'

[23]But he continued, 'You are from below; I am from above. You are of this world; I am not of this world. [24]I told you that you would die in your sins; if you do not believe

The radical solution

The climax of the story comes as Jesus makes another of those extraordinary statements about himself around which John's Gospel so often revolves. For he speaks of a time, as yet unknown to the woman, in which men and women would no longer be put right with God at specific places. The whole sacrificial system would be superseded. 'A time is coming', Jesus says, when those who seek to draw near to God will draw near to him in a new way. 'God is spirit,' he says, 'and his worshippers must worship in spirit and in truth' (4:23–24). At first, this seems to surprise the woman once more, and she responds by commenting that when the Messiah comes he will explain everything to her. Jesus replies: 'I who speak to you am he' (4:26).

The 'time' that Jesus refers to here is his own death on the cross.[7] It was that climactic moment to which his own life was heading and which would finally and for ever provide the solution to the problem that the woman – along with every single one of us – faces. For here Jesus Christ himself became the sacrifice for 'sin'. As John the Baptist had predicted when he described Jesus as 'the Lamb of God, who takes away the sin of the world' (1:29), his death was the 'sacrificial' means by which he took responsibility for every way in which you and I exclude God from our lives. What ultimately defaces and demeans our humanity is that we do not live as God intended. We choose to pursue our visions of life without reference to God and his purposes, and then wonder why our expectations of other people (and of ourselves) are so often disappointed.

The point of this particular episode, then, is that we will truly discover what it means to be human only in the same way that the woman did: by facing up to our own moral failures and asking for that forgiveness without which we will not know God. And – like the woman – we will come to that point only by means of a personal encounter with

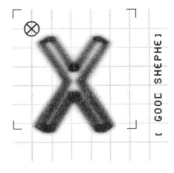

[30]

that I am [the one I claim to be], you will indeed die in your sins.'

²⁵'Who are you?' they asked.

'Just what I have been claiming all along,' Jesus replied. ²⁶'I have much to say in judgment of you. But he who sent me is reliable, and what I have heard from him I tell the world.'

²⁷They did not understand that he was telling them about his Father. ²⁸So Jesus said, 'When you have lifted up the Son of Man, then you will know that I am [the one I claim to be] and that I do nothing on my own but speak just what the Father has taught me. ²⁹The one who sent me is with me; he has not left me alone, for I always do what pleases him.' ³⁰Even as he spoke, many put their faith in him.

The children of Abraham

³¹To the Jews who had believed him, Jesus said, 'If you hold to my teaching, you are really my disciples. ³²Then you will know the truth, and the truth will set you free.'

³³They answered him, 'We are Abraham's descendants and have never been slaves of anyone. How can you say that we shall be set free?'

³⁴Jesus replied, 'I tell you the truth, everyone who sins is a slave to sin. ³⁵Now a slave has no permanent place in the family, but a son belongs to it for ever. ³⁶So if the Son sets you free, you will be free indeed. ³⁷I know you are Abraham's descendants. Yet you are ready to kill me, because you have no room for my word. ³⁸I am telling you what I have seen in the Father's presence, and you do what you have heard from your father.'

³⁹'Abraham is our father,' they answered.

'If you were Abraham's children,' said Jesus, 'then you would do the things Abraham did. ⁴⁰As it is, you are determined to kill me, a man who has told you the truth that I heard from God. Abraham did not do such things. ⁴¹You are doing the things your own father does.'

'We are not illegitimate children,' they

Jesus. To quote Pascal once more: 'Not only do we only know God through Jesus Christ, but we only know ourselves through Jesus Christ.'[8]

Who am I? The question at issue in this chapter has been inescapably personal. It is also highly contemporary. For we live in a culture which appears to be obsessed with a crisis of identity, and is at the same time completely unable to solve it. It is a situation which – as Peter Berger comments – is 'a condition conducive to considerable nervousness'.[9]

But … God still speaks.

[REAL LIVES]

ANDREW CHIANG

Andrew is in his third year of theological studies.

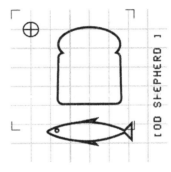

[GOD SHEPHERD]

[31]

Being born in the United Kingdom automatically made me a British citizen, but having grown up in a Christian home certainly did not guarantee that I would be a Christian. My father being a pastor and my mother a missionary inevitably made me susceptible to what some may consider religious brainwashing. However, throughout my childhood and adolescence I certainly resisted such 'indoctrination' in my life and protested. 'The only Father we have is God himself.'

The children of the devil

[42]Jesus said to them, 'If God were your Father, you would love me, for I came from God and now am here. I have not come on my own; but he sent me. [43]Why is my language not clear to you? Because you are unable to hear what I say. [44]You belong to your father, the devil, and you want to carry out your father's desire. He was a murderer from the beginning, not holding to the truth, for there is no truth in him. When he lies, he speaks his native language, for he is a liar and the father of lies. [45]Yet because I tell the truth, you do not believe me! [46]Can any of you prove me guilty of sin? If I am telling the truth, why don't you believe me? [47]Whoever belongs to God hears what God says. The reason you do not hear is that you do not belong to God.'

The claims of Jesus about himself

[48]The Jews answered him, 'Aren't we right in saying that you are a Samaritan and demon-possessed?'

[49]'I am not possessed by a demon,' said Jesus, 'but I honour my Father and you dishonour me. [50]I am not seeking glory for myself; but there is one who seeks it, and he is the judge. [51]I tell you the truth, whoever keeps my word will never see death.'

[52]At this the Jews exclaimed, 'Now we know that you are demon-possessed! Abraham died and so did the prophets, yet you say that whoever keeps your word will never taste death. [53]Are you greater than our father Abraham? He died, and so did the prophets. Who do you think you are?'

[54]Jesus replied, 'If I glorify myself, my glory means nothing. My Father, whom you claim as your God, is the one who glorifies me. [55]Though you do not know him, I know him. If I said I did not, I

behaviour, if not in my basic worldview. 'What does it mean for me to be a Christian?' was not something which I gave much thought to - I simply took it for granted as part of my cultural and intellectual identity. The central tenets of Christianity seemed to make sense - God died in the place of men and women, thus evidencing his love towards all humankind; I could accept this (and feel touched by it). But so what? Should not life go on just the same, regardless of what happened almost two millennia ago?

When I was seventeen, I attended a Christian camp over the Easter vacation. It involved, among other things, telling others about Christ through various activities such as drama, concerts, discos and evening meals. I went on this camp primarily to experience something different and to meet new friends (from all around the world). Over the period of seven days, my entire outlook on life changed dramatically. I realized that either I had to accept the claims of Christ as true, and hence live my life in a way fundamentally different from the way I had done; or I could choose to reject everything which I had believed up to that point. The living faith so evident in the lives of those I got to know influenced me profoundly. Was this what true Christianity is all about? Not just a set of beliefs, doctrines and tradition; nor the habitual repetition of church attendance and saying grace before a meal. What I had finally encountered was nothing less than an active, life-changing reality which could have come only from a living God - not a dead ideology.

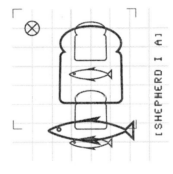

[SHEPHERD I A]

[32]

'I AM'

The way in which Jesus uses the phrase 'I am' has huge significance, given his Jewish context, and helps explain the degree of response it provoked. 'I am' was commonly a way of referring to God. It emphasized his eternal existence and his independence. Jesus boldly makes the phrase his own and allows people to draw their own conclusions about who he claims to be. 'I am' focused minds on God's distinctiveness. Jesus unashamedly asserts that he shares these distinctives.

would be a liar like you, but I do know him and keep his word. ⁵⁶Your father Abraham rejoiced at the thought of seeing my day; he saw it and was glad.'

⁵⁷'You are not yet fifty years old,' the Jews said to him, 'and you have seen Abraham!'

⁵⁸'I tell you the truth,' Jesus answered, 'before Abraham was born, I am!' ⁵⁹At this, they picked up stones to stone him, but Jesus hid himself, slipping away from the temple grounds.

Since that Easter my worldview has changed. The historical truth of Christ's resurrection was no longer a mere fact, but an event which radically transformed my life, and the lives of all who confess Christ as their Lord and Saviour. I was no longer to be the centre of my life -rather, Christ alone would take that position. If God is creator and sustainer of this world, then as a child of God (since all Christians are God's children), I should lack nothing. I did not need to keep pursuing my own goals, striving for my own selfish ambitions, because all I could ever require God would provide. Instead I could, in perfect assurance, seek to live for God, obeying his commands, knowing that what God wants is always (God being a God of unconditional love) what is best for myself, my family and friends, my country and all humanity.

Christians are not distinct from other people psychologically, intellectually, socially, physiologically or aesthetically; rather, they are different because they have a living hope within them, a faith in an infinite yet personal God, and the experience of true, unconditional love. This is now what it means for me to be a Christian.

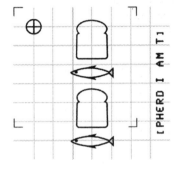

[33]

CHAPTER **[9]**

Jesus heals a man born blind

[1]As he went along, he saw a man blind from birth. [2]His disciples asked him, 'Rabbi, who sinned, this man or his parents, that he was born blind?'

[3]'Neither this man nor his parents sinned,' said Jesus, 'but this happened so that the work of God might be displayed in his life. [4]As long as it is day, we must do the work of him who sent me. Night is coming, when no-one can work. [5]While I am in the world, I am the light of the world.'

[6]Having said this, he spat on the ground, made some mud with the saliva, and put it on the man's eyes. [7]'Go,' he told him, 'wash in the Pool of Siloam' (this word means Sent). So the man went and washed, and came home seeing.

[8]His neighbours and those who had formerly seen him begging asked, 'Isn't this the same man who used to sit and beg?' [9]Some claimed that he was.

Others said, 'No, he only looks like him.' But he himself insisted, 'I am the man.'

[3] Who's in control?

'What is good? Everything that heightens the feeling of power in man, the will to power, power itself.'
  FRIEDRICH NIETZSCHE, *THE ANTICHRIST*

'Power is the ultimate aphrodisiac.'
  HENRY KISSINGER

'The power of man has grown in every sphere, except over himself.'
  SIR WINSTON CHURCHILL

'Big brother'

The recent film *Enemy of the State* portrays a nightmarish scenario where the central character (played by Will Smith) is hounded by the 'security' services after he unknowingly becomes the plant for a computer disk portraying the murder of a leading politician. The politician had refused to vote for an increase in the level of surveillance being imposed on

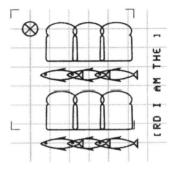

[34]

¹⁰'How then were your eyes opened?' they demanded.

¹¹He replied, 'The man they call Jesus made some mud and put it on my eyes. He told me to go to Siloam and wash. So I went and washed, and then I could see.'

¹²'Where is this man?' they asked him.

'I don't know,' he said.

The Pharisees investigate the healing

¹³They brought to the Pharisees the man who had been blind. ¹⁴Now the day on which Jesus had made the mud and opened the man's eyes was a Sabbath. ¹⁵Therefore the Pharisees also asked him how he had received his sight. 'He put mud on my eyes,' the man replied, 'and I washed, and now I see.'

¹⁶Some of the Pharisees said, 'This man is not from God, for he does not keep the Sabbath.'

But others asked, 'How can a sinner do such miraculous signs?' So they were divided.

¹⁷Finally they turned again to the blind man, 'What have you to say about him? It was your eyes he opened.'

The man replied, 'He is a prophet.'

¹⁸The Jews still did not believe that he had been blind and had received his sight until they sent for the man's parents. ¹⁹'Is this your son?' they asked. 'Is this the one you say was born blind? How is it that now he can see?'

²⁰'We know he is our son,' the parents answered, 'and we know he was born blind. ²¹But how he can see now, or who opened his eyes, we don't know. Ask him. He is of age; he will speak for himself.' ²²His parents said this because they were afraid of the Jews, for already the Jews had decided that anyone who acknowledged that Jesus was the Christ would be put out of the synagogue. ²³That was why his parents said, 'He is of age; ask him.'

²⁴A second time they summoned the man who had been blind. 'Give glory to God,' they said. 'We know this man is a sinner.'

citizens. His murderer is one of the heads of the security service itself, and Smith's character's life is turned inside out as he spends most of the film on the run from the intrusive ability of the security service to keep tabs on his every move. His phone is tapped, his roadside calls are traced, his clothing is bugged, his watch has a transistor planted in it, his home is wired. There appears to be no way out, until – in partnership with an ex-surveillance officer – he turns the tables on his assailants by beginning to use the weapons that have been used on him to expose them.

Films like this remind us that in our high-tech world, there are highly sinister aspects to the potential use of power – even within what we imagine to be a democratic and free society where individuals suppose that they enjoy certain 'inalienable' human rights and are free from outside intrusion. But the film is symptomatic also of a wider unease in our society about the use of power. We are increasingly suspicious today of those who wield power, be they politicians, spin-doctors or advertisers. We begin to feel sometimes that our lives are beyond our control; that maybe we are simply victims of competing groups; that our lives are at the mercy of other people's vested interests for power.

On a wider scale, many of the movements in our own generation can be seen in the context of a reaction against this sort of repression. The women's liberation movement has reacted against the domination of men in social, political and family life. The civil rights movement in the United States sought to obtain for blacks the rights which whites had taken for granted, and which they had sometimes used as grounds for the expression of racial superiority and even subjugation of blacks. The movement for democracy in Eastern Europe over the last decade was at heart a reaction against the totalitarianism of the communist régimes which had all but extinguished the democratic expression of freedom.

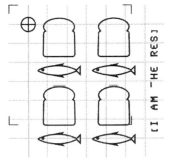

[35]

[25]He replied, 'Whether he is a sinner or not, I don't know. One thing I do know.

I was blind but now I see!'

[26]Then they asked him, 'What did he do to you? How did he open your eyes?'

[27]He answered, 'I have told you already and you did not listen. Why do you want to hear it again? Do you want to become his disciples, too?'

[28]Then they hurled insults at him and said, 'You are this fellow's disciple! We are disciples of Moses! [29]We know that God spoke to Moses, but as for this fellow, we don't even know where he comes from.'

[30]The man answered, 'Now that is remarkable! You don't know where he comes from, yet he opened my eyes. [31]We know that God does not listen to sinners. He listens to the godly person who does his will. [32]Nobody has ever heard of opening the eyes of someone born blind. [33]If this man were not from God, he could do nothing.'

[34]To this they replied, 'You were steeped in sin at birth; how dare you lecture us!' And they threw him out.

The power of ideology

In this bigger picture it is not only individuals and organizations that have come under suspicion, but more fundamentally those ideologies that inform and fuel their activities: communism, imperialism, patriarchalism and so on. In our postmodern world, these are some of the 'metanarratives' (the grand ideas) about which contemporary thinkers are most suspicious. For in the end, so it is argued, the exercise of power by those under the control of such ideologies has often led to the coercion or repression of other people, nearly always in the minority.

As a Christian, I need to face the fact that this charge has often rightly been made about Christians and about the church. For hasn't Christianity been responsible for some outrageous acts of repression in history? Hasn't Christianity often been used as a cloak for the acquisition of power? Or on a more individual level, haven't Christians often used a powerful message (with a threat hanging over those who reject it) as an excuse to manipulate those who are weak into some sort of profession of faith?

Power and the individual

We cannot escape the question of power, therefore. For whether on a national, corporate or individual level, we deal with it all the time. So can Christianity defend itself against the charges brought? And more than that, can it give some answers to the questions that the issue of power raises?

The issue of power appears at various points in the Gospel of John. And nowhere are these issues presented more sharply than in his portrayal of the way in which Jesus gets killed. For here the exercise of religious power – in judging and finally condemning him to death – serves to highlight not only the corporate and individual aspects of power, but

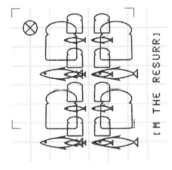

[36]

Spiritual blindness

[35]Jesus heard that they had thrown him out, and when he found him, he said, 'Do you believe in the Son of Man?'

[36]'Who is he, sir?' the man asked. 'Tell me so that I may believe in him.'

[37]Jesus said, 'You have now seen him; in fact, he is the one speaking with you.'

[38]Then the man said, 'Lord, I believe,' and he worshipped him.

[39]Jesus said, 'For judgment I have come into this world, so that the blind will see and those who see will become blind.'

[40]Some Pharisees who were with him heard him say this and asked, 'What? Are we blind too?'

[41]Jesus said, 'If you were blind, you would not be guilty of sin; but now that you claim you can see, your guilt remains.

John 9:35-41

also the much greater cosmic confrontation of which these are a part. It also radically subverts the view that Christianity is at heart about the repression of others by the use of power. So how does John do this?

Jesus and power

The first thing to note is the way in which John emphasizes Jesus' own personal power. We're not surprised by this, of course. He is recorded as doing miracles of power in almost every chapter. What's more, we're told that this power is perceived by onlookers to have a divine origin. As Nicodemus says to Jesus: 'Rabbi, we know you are a teacher who has come from God. For you could not perform the miraculous signs you are doing if God were not with you' (3:2). As if to confirm this coming together of power and divinity, two of the titles most frequently used of Jesus in John's Gospel are 'Lord' (thirty-six times) and 'King' (sixteen times). Both imply power and authority and both are scattered throughout the narrative. The first reaches its climax at the resurrection scene, where Thomas ('doubting' Thomas, as history has come to know him) eventually meets the risen Jesus and is invited to put his finger into the wounds that had been sustained three days earlier at the crucifixion. With sudden realization, Thomas falls at Jesus' feet to worship him, and calls him 'My Lord and my God' (20:28).

The title 'King' is first used in chapter 1, where Nathanael, having just met Jesus, says to him, 'Rabbi, you are the Son of God; you are the King of Israel' (1:49). This statement acts almost like an overture to the Gospel, introducing a highly significant theme as far as John is concerned. It next crops up in chapter 6, after Jesus has made enough food from a boy's picnic lunch to feed over 5,000 people. In a setting of heightened messianic expectation, the crowd at once latches on to the potential significance of what he has done. For, like a

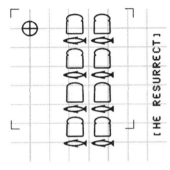

[THE RESURRECT]

[37]

In earlier Jewish writings, leaders among the people were sometimes pictured as shepherds caring for a flock. This found a particular focus in the king and looked forward to the promised ruler (see note on 'Messiah', 4:25). Jesus takes up this image to compare his leadership with the inadequacies of the leaders of his time. They are pictured as thieves, robbers and strangers, failing to provide proper care. Jesus is pictured as the good shepherd or perfect ruler caring for his sheep, bringing them life and protection. He will even give his life for the sheep.

CHAPTER [10]

The shepherd and his flock

[1]'I tell you the truth, anyone who does not enter the sheep pen by the gate, but climbs in by some other way, is a thief and a robber. [2]The one who enters by the gate is the shepherd of his sheep. [3]The gatekeeper opens the gate for him, and the sheep listen to his voice. He calls his own sheep by name and leads them out. [4]When he has brought out all his own, he goes on ahead of them, and his sheep follow him because they know his voice. [5]But they will never follow a stranger; in fact, they will run away from him because they do not recognise a stranger's voice.' [6]Jesus used this figure of speech, but they did not understand what he was telling them.

[7]Therefore Jesus said again, 'I tell you the truth, I am the gate for the sheep. [8]All who ever came before me were thieves and robbers, but the sheep did not listen to them. [9]I am the gate; all who enter through me will be saved. They will come in and go out, and find pasture. [10]The thief

previous 'deliverer', Moses, who produced manna, Jesus has fed his people in the wilderness. Here, they believe, is another Moses, a political leader and deliverer, not this time from the slavery of Egypt, but from the yoke of the Romans, the occupying power. Let's crown him, they enthuse, proclaim him as king and – with over 5,000 potential rebels in tow – who knows, maybe even overthrow the oppressor. But Jesus, 'knowing that they intended to come and make him king by force', immediately rejects such militaristic plans, and 'withdrew again to a mountain by himself' (6:15).

Coercion?

Here then is an important angle on the question of power in John's Gospel: for Jesus refuses the role of a military and political deliverer. He will not be used to secure purely political ends, and will not entertain for a moment the thought that coercion for such ends is what he – as King – has come to achieve.

This theme re-emerges at the trial scene, where Jesus is confronted by a 'real' king, Pontius Pilate, the Roman Governor of Judea. 'Are you the king of the Jews?' he asks Jesus (18:33). Pilate is intrigued, yet also seriously worried by the potential threat he perceives to come from the man standing in front of him. Jesus has gained an enormous popular following and is presented by the religious authorities as a power-usurper. 'My kingdom is not of this world,' replies Jesus. 'If it were, my servants would fight to prevent my arrest by the Jews. But … my kingdom is from another place' (18:36).

According to Jesus, his kingship is not earthly in the sense of originating in the ideas or plans of human beings. It is not about earthly kingdoms and ruling power. The potentially revolutionary outcome of the feeding miracle (chapter 6) decided that issue. No, the kingship that Jesus has come to demonstrate and exercise is of a different order

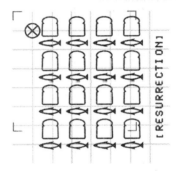

[38]

comes only to steal and kill and destroy; I have come that they may have life, and have it to the full.

¹¹'I am the good shepherd. The good shepherd lays down his life for the sheep. ¹²The hired hand is not the shepherd who owns the sheep. So when he sees the wolf coming, he abandons the sheep and runs away. Then the wolf attacks the flock and scatters it. ¹³The man runs away because he is a hired hand and cares nothing for the sheep.

¹⁴'I am the good shepherd; I know my sheep and my sheep know me – ¹⁵just as the Father knows me and I know the Father – and I lay down my life for the sheep. ¹⁶I have other sheep that are not of this sheep pen. I must bring them also. They too will listen to my voice, and there shall be one flock and one shepherd. ¹⁷The reason my Father loves me is that I lay down my life – only to take it up again. ¹⁸No-one takes it from me, but I lay it down of my own accord. I have authority to lay it down and authority to take it up again. This command I received from my Father.'

¹⁹At these words the Jews were again divided. ²⁰Many of them said, 'He is demon-possessed and raving mad. Why listen to him?'

²¹But others said, 'These are not the sayings of someone possessed by a demon. Can a demon open the eyes of the blind?'

The unbelief of the Jews

²²Then came the Feast of Dedication at Jerusalem. It was winter, ²³and Jesus was in the temple area walking in Solomon's Colonnade. ²⁴The Jews gathered round him, saying, 'How long will you keep us in suspense? If you are the Christ, tell us plainly.'

²⁵Jesus answered, 'I did tell you, but you do not believe. The miracles I do in my Father's name speak for me, ²⁶but you do not believe because you are not my sheep. ²⁷My sheep listen to my voice; I know them, and they follow me. ²⁸I give them eternal

altogether. It has to do not with coercion for the sake of power itself (eat your heart out, Nietzsche), but with a battle which will finally establish the true protagonists in the power struggle, and will also establish the true victor.

'You are a king, then!' says Pilate.

'You are right in saying I am a king,' Jesus answers. 'In fact, for this reason I was born, and for this I came into the world, to testify to the truth. Everyone on the side of truth listens to me' (18:37).

Pilate, however, has seriously lost the plot at this point (if not long before). He cannot begin to fathom what Jesus is speaking about, and becomes increasingly agitated. 'Don't you realise I have power either to free you or to crucify you?', he exclaims (19:10) – half muscle-flexing, half hoping (even pleading?) that Jesus will even now submit to his own version of 'power'. But Jesus, though seen by the reader at this point as almost inevitably the eventual victim of Pilate's fear, emphatically puts Pilate's own power in its true context. 'You would have no power over me', says Jesus, 'if it were not given to you from above' (19:11).

Power crucified

Finally, Pilate himself becomes (without knowing it) the mouthpiece at the crucifixion itself for the truth about power and where it operates. For when Jesus is nailed to the cross, Pilate has a title board prepared to fix above Jesus' head. On it are written the words: 'JESUS OF NAZARETH, THE KING OF THE JEWS' (19:19). It proclaims its message as widely as possible: in Aramaic (the common language), in Latin (the language of government), and in Greek (the language of trade and commerce). The chief priests protest, arguing that Jesus only 'claimed' that he was the king of the Jews, but Pilate dismisses their objection and

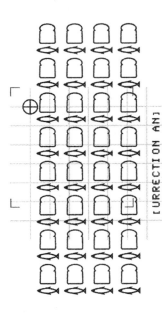

[39]

OUTRAGE

The story unfolds widespread confusion about and growing animosity towards Jesus. This now takes a more sinister turn. Accused of claiming to be God, Jesus is threatened first by stoning and then by arrest. His claim is to be 'one with the Father', which suggests both equality and identity – there is nothing about the character of Jesus which is not also true about God. This outrageous claim is seized upon by those listening as a legitimate reason for summary justice.

life, and they shall never perish; no-one can snatch them out of my hand. 29My Father, who has given them to me, is greater than all; no-one can snatch them out of my Father's hand. 30I and the Father are one.'

31Again the Jews picked up stones to stone him, 32but Jesus said to them, 'I have shown you many great miracles from the Father. For which of these do you stone me?'

33'We are not stoning you for any of these,' replied the Jews, 'but for blasphemy, because you, a mere human being, claim to be God.'

34Jesus answered them, 'Is it not written in your Law, "I have said you are gods"? 35If he called them "gods", to whom the word of God came – and the Scripture cannot be broken – 36what about the one whom the Father set apart as his very own and sent into the world? Why then do you accuse me of blasphemy because I said, "I am God's Son"? 37Do not believe me unless I do what my Father does. 38But if I do it, even though you do not believe me, believe the miracles, that you may know and understand that the Father is in me, and I in the Father.' 39Again they tried to seize him, but he escaped their grasp.

40Then Jesus went back across the Jordan to the place where John had been baptising in the early days. Here he stayed 41and many people came to him. They said, 'Though John never performed a miraculous sign, all that John said about this man was true.' 42And in that place many believed in Jesus.

answers, 'What I have written, I have written' (19:22). In other words, by putting up the display in these three languages, Pilate looks to ridicule Jesus' power claims in the most emphatic way possible. Here is 'power' he says, and see what it looks like.

But perhaps the major irony of the Gospel of John is that Pilate is indeed here stating the absolute truth about this man Jesus. For the Gospel of John subverts all known interpretations and expressions of power. It is on the cross, argues John, in all its apparent weakness and *lack* of power, that Jesus most clearly expresses his kingship.

The crucifixion of Jesus is not a display of power as this world conceives of power. It has nothing to do with the coercion of others in human terms, nothing to do with manipulation – at least as far as Jesus Christ manipulating others is concerned. After all, it is Jesus who is being crucified here, not other people. If you had been standing at the foot of the cross and had been asked to identify the 'powerful' agents in the drama, it would not have crossed your mind to suggest that this weak, dying man was occupying a place of any power at all.

This, of course, has enormous implications for one of the questions we raised at the outset. For no matter how Christianity has been viewed in the past, or however Christians have appeared to come across to others, the 'power' at the heart of its message is one that is 'crucified'. In whatever sense we understand this act to be an expression of 'power', it is power – as we shall see – which is placed at the service of others.

The cross and true power

Something far more subtle, then, is going on here: subtle, and yet clear and powerful enough to send Christians into the ancient (and the contemporary) world with a message about liberation and about freedom.

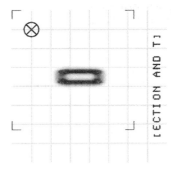

[40]

CHAPTER [11]

The death of Lazarus

¹Now a man named Lazarus was sick. He was from Bethany, the village of Mary and her sister Martha. ²This Mary, whose brother Lazarus now lay sick, was the same one who poured perfume on the Lord and wiped his feet with her hair. ³So the sisters sent word to Jesus, 'Lord, the one you love is sick.'

⁴When he heard this, Jesus said, 'This sickness will not end in death. No, it is for God's glory so that God's Son may be glorified through it.' ⁵Jesus loved Martha and her sister and Lazarus. ⁶Yet when he heard that Lazarus was sick, he stayed where he was two more days.

⁷Then he said to his disciples, 'Let us go back to Judea.'

⁸'But Rabbi,' they said, 'a short while ago the Jews tried to stone you, and yet you are going back there?'

⁹Jesus answered, 'Are there not twelve hours of daylight? Those who walk by day will not stumble, for they see by this world's

So what precisely is going on here?

John is eager to tell us. Even at the crucifixion scene, there are some telling clues. In the first place, there is the continual reference to the fact that somehow or other, some text of the Old Testament is being fulfilled by the seemingly insignificant details of what is going on.

- When the soldiers hesitate to tear Jesus' clothes in order to get a piece each, we are told: 'This happened that the scripture might be fulfilled which said, "They divided my garments among them and cast lots for my clothing"' (19:24).

- John says, 'Later, knowing that all was now completed, and so that the Scripture would be fulfilled, Jesus said, "I am thirsty"' (19:28).

- John records why the soldiers broke the legs of the other criminals but not those of Jesus: 'These things happened so that the scripture would be fulfilled: "Not one of his bones will be broken," and, as another scripture says, "They will look on the one they have pierced"' (19:36–37).

John presents the case that what is happening to Jesus on the cross – awful as it appears – is not some dreadful mistake. In fact, extraordinarily, it fulfils God's intentions. It is the culmination of the statement that 'God so loved the world that he gave his one and only Son' (3:16). He is involved personally in this event in a way that brings his plans for the world to fulfilment by 'giving' his Son, even to die.

Moreover, Jesus himself is fully committed to this course of action. He is both fully involved and fully willing to go through with it. He makes it quite clear that he personally

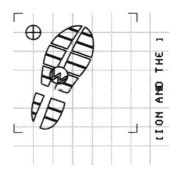

[41]

light. ¹⁰It is when they walk by night that they stumble, for they have no light.'

¹¹After he had said this, he went on to tell them, 'Our friend Lazarus has fallen asleep; but I am going there to wake him up.'

¹²His disciples replied, 'Lord, if he sleeps, he will get better.' ¹³Jesus had been speaking of his death, but his disciples thought he meant natural sleep.

¹⁴So then he told them plainly, 'Lazarus is dead, ¹⁵and for your sake I am glad I was not there, so that you may believe. But let us go to him.'

¹⁶Then Thomas (called Didymus) said to the rest of the disciples, 'Let us also go, that we may die with him.'

Jesus comforts the sisters

¹⁷On his arrival, Jesus found that Lazarus had already been in the tomb for four days. ¹⁸Bethany was less than two miles from Jerusalem, ¹⁹and many Jews had come to Martha and Mary to comfort them in the loss of their brother. ²⁰When Martha heard that Jesus was coming, she went out to meet him, but Mary stayed at home.

²¹'Lord,' Martha said to Jesus, 'if you had been here, my brother would not have died. ²²But I know that even now God will give you whatever you ask.'

²³Jesus said to her, 'Your brother will rise again.'

²⁴Martha answered, 'I know he will rise again in the resurrection at the last day.'

²⁵Jesus said to her, 'I am the resurrection and the life. Those who believe in me will live, even though they die; ²⁶and whoever lives and believes in me will never die. Do you believe this?'

²⁷'Yes, Lord,' she told him, 'I believe that you are the Christ, the Son of God, who was to come into the world.'

²⁸And after she had said this, she went back and called her sister Mary aside. 'The Teacher is here,' she said, 'and is asking for you.' ²⁹When Mary heard this, she got up quickly and went to him. ³⁰Now Jesus had not yet entered the village, but was still at

is in charge of his own destiny and that he fully agrees with God's plan for his life. 'The reason my Father loves me', he says, 'is that I lay down my life – only to take it up again. No-one takes it from me, but I lay it down of my own accord. I have authority to lay it down and authority to take it up again. This command I received from my Father' (10:17–18).

At the crucifixion scene, too, John builds into the narrative a heavy sense of irony. The interplay in the verbs and objects is not coincidental. At one level the power resides with Jesus' opponents. 'Pilate handed him over to them to be crucified. So the soldiers took charge of Jesus' (19:16). 'They crucified him' (19:18). But at another level Jesus himself shows the real power. It is he who really controls what goes on. Not only does he carry his own cross (19:17); he also retains the consciousness to 'know' what is going on, and therefore to 'control' events in an appropriate way (e.g. 19:28). Finally, it is he who draws things to closure with the statement of achievement, 'It is finished' (19:30). And – in the context of a chapter all about others crucifying him – it is significant that it is Jesus who 'bowed his head and gave up his spirit' (19:30), not others who take his life from him.

The ultimate power encounter

If we are to understand the cross of Jesus (and therefore understand the message that John is communicating), we have to understand what Jesus himself says about its meaning. He gives us the inside track. Referring to his coming death, he says: 'Now is the time for judgment on this world; now the prince of this world will be driven out. But I, when I am lifted up from the earth, will draw all people to myself ' (12:31–32).

According to these words of Jesus, two things of monumental significance are taking place as he is 'lifted up' on to the cross to die.

First, he says, it is about a power encounter. But ultimately his crucifixion is not an

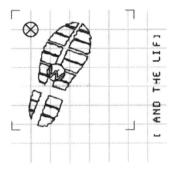

[AND THE LIFE]

[42]

the place where Martha had met him. ³¹When the Jews who had been with Mary in the house, comforting her, noticed how quickly she got up and went out, they followed her, supposing she was going to the tomb to mourn there.

³²When Mary reached the place where Jesus was and saw him, she fell at his feet and said, 'Lord, if you had been here, my brother would not have died.'

³³When Jesus saw her weeping, and the Jews who had come along with her also weeping, he was deeply moved in spirit and troubled. ³⁴'Where have you laid him?' he asked.

'Come and see, Lord,' they replied.

³⁵Jesus wept.

³⁶Then the Jews said, 'See how he loved him!'

³⁷But some of them said, 'Could not he who opened the eyes of the blind man have kept this man from dying?'

Jesus raises Lazarus from the dead

³⁸Jesus, once more deeply moved, came to the tomb. It was a cave with a stone laid across the entrance. ³⁹'Take away the stone,' he said.

'But, Lord,' said Martha, the sister of the dead man, 'by this time there is a bad odour, for he has been there four days.'

⁴⁰Then Jesus said, 'Did I not tell you that if you believed, you would see the glory of God?'

⁴¹So they took away the stone. Then Jesus looked up and said, 'Father, I thank you that you have heard me. ⁴²I knew that you always hear me, but I said this for the benefit of the people standing here, that they may believe that you sent me.'

encounter with human power – even though Pilate and the religious authorities play such a prominent human role in the proceedings. No, the primary battle here, says Jesus, is with the power behind human evil: behind every unjust, cruel or illegal display of power in the history of the world. This is the power that is being 'driven out': a personal manifestation of evil that Jesus describes as 'the prince of this world'.

But how is he driven out by Jesus? By the fact that Jesus' death (and his subsequent rising to a new life three days later) would demonstrate once and for all that 'the prince of this world' had no power over him. For every attempt by the evil one to nail Jesus (and finish him) by identifying within him an evil inclination, or an evil thought, or an evil reaction, would be shown to have come to nothing. He was killed – yes, but death could not overpower him. For the evil which alone could have kept him there was altogether absent from Jesus. This is the true irony of what is going on at the death of Jesus. What looked for all the world like the most ignominious defeat, turns out to be the most awesome victory.

Perhaps you've been reading this chapter and thinking that somehow you operate outside the sphere in which this power encounter is taking place. Perhaps you feel that your life is not touched by evil. Not so, says Jesus. And the fact that you will not break the barrier of death by rising from it – as Jesus did – will one day prove it. Our daily lives show that our own reactions, thoughts and inclinations are so often basically self-centred and inward-facing. The fact that we do give in to (or are overpowered by) reactions, thoughts and intentions that are not true, or loving, or just, simply goes to prove it. We do not respond to God's desires and invitations, not so much because we are apathetic, but because we lack the will to do what is right.

What John does is to take this fact and focus it precisely in our reaction at this moment

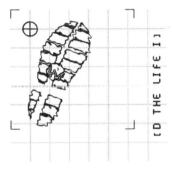

[43]

[43]When he had said this, Jesus called in a loud voice,

'Lazarus, come out!'

John 11:43

of our lives to this man Jesus. John puts it this way: 'This is the verdict: Light has come into the world, but people loved darkness instead of light because their deeds were evil' (3:19). The 'light' referred to here is Jesus himself: and the fact that we have not responded to his light and turned to him for forgiveness and new life is symptomatic of the fact that our deeds, thoughts and actions are 'evil'.

So we cannot excuse ourselves in this grim scenario. We are implicated. We are guilty. And our guilt is exposed by our reaction to Jesus himself, the purest light that ever entered our dark world.

The victory of the cross

The second thing that Jesus says about his death, therefore, is that because of it individuals can be brought back to the friendship and safety of Jesus himself. 'But I,' he says, 'when I am lifted up from the earth, will draw all people to myself' (12:31). As we have seen, when Jesus is 'lifted up' on to the cross in death, the evil one is ultimately disempowered and shown to be the loser. As a result, those in his service can become the subjects of a greater power by being rescued from his grip. Present allies of 'the prince of this world' can be drawn away from his power into the company and friendship of the true King, Jesus. That is why Jesus says: 'I tell you the truth, those who hear my word and believe him who sent me have eternal life and will not be condemned; they have crossed over from death to life' (5:24).

To respond to this invitation brings us 'life' in the sense that we will be forgiven for those things which otherwise would condemn us and kill us eternally, and it unites us for ever to Jesus himself, so that all that he has done for us can be made effective in our own lives.

Perhaps a picture will help. I can remember flicking channels and coming across a

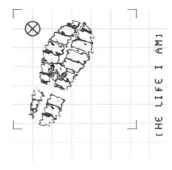

[THE LIFE I AM]

[44]

Lazarus, dead for four days, is brought back to life by Jesus. John clearly presents this as an historical event demonstrating a fundamental truth. It is told to substantiate Jesus Christ's claim that he will give life to people beyond death. This miracle is a test case, showing Jesus' power to bring someone back to life. It demonstrates his ability to shatter the grim hold of death. He promises to accomplish that for all who believe in him.

[44] The dead man came out, his hands and feet wrapped with strips of linen, and a cloth around his face.

Jesus said to them, 'Take off the grave clothes and let him go.'

The plot to kill Jesus

[45] Therefore many of the Jews who had come to visit Mary, and had seen what Jesus did, put their faith in him. [46] But some of them went to the Pharisees and told them what Jesus had done. [47] Then the chief priests and the Pharisees called a meeting of the Sanhedrin.

'What are we accomplishing?' they asked. 'Here is this man performing many miraculous signs. [48] If we let him go on like this, everyone will believe in him, and then the Romans will come and take away both our place and our nation.'

[49] Then one of them, named Caiaphas, who was high priest that year, spoke up, 'You know nothing at all! [50] You do not realise that it is better for you that one person die for the people than that the whole nation perish.'

[51] He did not say this on his own, but as high priest that year he prophesied that Jesus would die for the Jewish nation, [52] and not only for that nation but also for the scattered children of God, to bring them together and make them one. [53] So from that day on they plotted to take his life.

[54] Therefore Jesus no longer moved about publicly among the Jews. Instead he withdrew to a region near the desert, to a village called Ephraim, where he stayed with his disciples.

[55] When it was almost time for the Jewish Passover, many went up from the country to Jerusalem for their ceremonial cleansing before the Passover. [56] They kept looking for Jesus, and as they stood in the temple area they asked one another, 'What do you think? Isn't he coming to the Feast at all?' [57] But the chief priests and Pharisees had given orders that if anyone found out where Jesus was, he should report it so that they might arrest him.

scene from an old western movie. The scene was filled with a stagecoach in distress. It was hurtling along with its occupants helpless to do anything because the axle had been fractured. Both wheels were still intact, but the camera angle suggested (none too subtly) that this situation was not going to last for much longer. Then into the frame another stagecoach appears, driven by the film's hero, who manages to manoeuvre it in a cloud of noise and dust alongside the first coach. In what turns out to be the climax of the film, our hero manages to pull out each of the occupants and bring them across to safety in his own carriage just before the first coach hits a rock and is smashed to pieces.

I'm not suggesting for one moment that John's Gospel is a B movie, but the scene here is at least analogous. We too are rushing headlong towards oblivion – says John – because we continuously ally ourselves with the force behind every manifestation of evil in our world. We may do this to a greater or lesser extent, but all of us are personally part of a world which has rejected the light of the good news that Jesus brings, and we show it by our thoughts and actions. Nevertheless, of his own volition – and at supreme personal cost to himself – Jesus does not leave us to this oblivion but comes alongside to pull us out of the impending wreckage and bring us into the safe haven of his protective care.

So in his treatment of the question of 'power', John puts it into the context of the greatest power struggle that has ever taken place: the battle between what is ultimately good and true and that which is ultimately degraded and evil. Throughout his gospel – but supremely in his death on the cross – John portrays Jesus engaging an enemy power and ultimately emerging victorious in a cosmic power encounter that transcends and eclipses every human power encounter that there has ever been – before or since. As a result of it, a number of things follow which will take us the rest of our lives to live out and respond to. For every interpretation and every use of power must now be judged in the

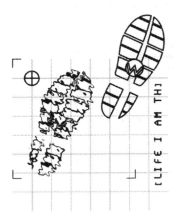

[45]

CHAPTER [12]

Jesus anointed at Bethany

[1]Six days before the Passover, Jesus arrived at Bethany, where Lazarus lived, whom Jesus had raised from the dead. [2]Here a dinner was given in Jesus' honour. Martha served, while Lazarus was among those reclining at the table with him. [3]Then Mary took about a pint of pure nard, an expensive perfume; she poured it on Jesus' feet and wiped his feet with her hair. And the house was filled with the fragrance of the perfume.

[4]But one of his disciples, Judas Iscariot, who was later to betray him, objected, [5]'Why wasn't this perfume sold and the money given to the poor? It was worth a year's wages.' [6]He did not say this because he cared about the poor but because he was a thief; as keeper of the money bag, he used to help himself to what was put into it.

[7]'Leave her alone,' Jesus replied. '[It was intended] that she should save this perfume for the day of my burial. [8]You will always have the poor among you, but you will not always have me.'

light of Jesus Christ. Is it being used for the service of others, or is it ultimately self-serving? Does it lead to true justice, or does it actually promote injustice and error? Is it seeking to establish political or economic power without reference to God's desires, or does it evaluate everything in the light of God's truth? And so on …

Whose side are you on?

But the place at which we must start in all this is the place where we declare our allegiance to one side or the other in the ultimate battle. There is, of course, nothing we can offer to this battle except the accumulating evidence that shows that we are naturally and habitually on the wrong side. There is nothing we can do to transfer ourselves from one side to the other in our own strength. No, the stakes with which Jesus plays are far too high. In fact, they are completely beyond our ability to contribute. All we can do is to respond to what Jesus has done for us, supremely on the cross. For if, by his death, Jesus is engaging and overcoming the ultimate power of evil in the world today, and he is doing it on my behalf, then the question with which I am left is simply this: will I be rescued? For how we respond to Jesus determines whose side we're on.

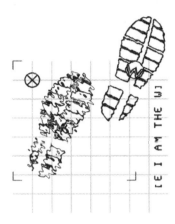

[46]

9Meanwhile a large crowd of Jews found out that Jesus was there and came, not only because of him but also to see Lazarus, whom he had raised from the dead. 10So the chief priests made plans to kill Lazarus as well, 11for on account of him many of the Jews were going over to Jesus and putting their faith in him.

The triumphal entry

12The next day the great crowd that had come for the Feast heard that Jesus was on his way to Jerusalem. 13They took palm branches and went out to meet him, shouting,

'Hosanna!'

'Blessed is he who comes in the name of the Lord!'

'Blessed is the King of Israel!'

14Jesus found a young donkey and sat upon it, as it is written,

15'Do not be afraid, O Daughter of Zion;
    see, your king is coming,
      seated on a donkey's colt.'

16At first his disciples did not understand all this. Only after Jesus was glorified did they realise that these things had been written about him and that they had done these things to him. 17Now the crowd that was with him when he called Lazarus from the tomb and raised him from the dead continued to spread the word. 18Many people, because they had heard that he had given this miraculous sign, went out to meet him. 19So the Pharisees said to one another, 'See, this is getting us nowhere. Look how the whole world has gone after him!'

Jesus predicts his death

20Now there were some Greeks among those who went up to worship at the Feast. 21They came to Philip, who was from Bethsaida in Galilee, with a request. 'Sir,'

[REAL LIVES]

HELEN RICHARDSON

Helen is in her second year of training in medicine.

Getting right with God is all about being good and doing as you're told, isn't it? Well, that's the impression I had for several years. I don't come from a Christian family, but I did go to Sunday school as a child, so I grew up knowing a fair amount about Christianity - or so I thought. When I was twelve, there were some confirmation classes running at my local church for those who wanted to make a real commitment to Jesus. To be honest, the main reason I went at all was that some of my friends were going and I didn't want to be left out! However, at one of these sessions, the vicar asked us why God should let us into heaven when we don't meet his standards. Then it suddenly hit me that there was nothing I could do to earn my way into God's good books - even as an arrogant pre-teenager, I didn't think I was perfect! Fortunately, the conversation didn't end there, and I found out that if I asked Jesus into my life I could be made right with God - not because of anything I've done but because Jesus died for me on the cross.

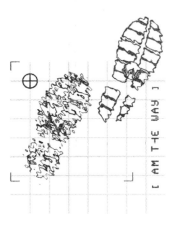

[47]

they said, 'we would like to see Jesus.' 22Philip went to tell Andrew; Andrew and Philip in turn told Jesus.

23Jesus replied, 'The hour has come for the Son of Man to be glorified. 24I tell you the truth, unless a grain of wheat falls to the ground and dies, it remains only a single seed. But if it dies, it produces many seeds. 25Those who love their lives will lose them, while those who hate their lives in this world will keep them for eternal life. 26Whoever serves me must follow me; and where I am, my servant also will be. My Father will honour the one who serves me.

27'Now my heart is troubled, and what shall I say? "Father, save me from this hour"? No, it was for this very reason I came to this hour. 28Father, glorify your name!'

Then a voice came from heaven, 'I have glorified it, and will glorify it again.' 29The crowd that was there and heard it said it had thundered; others said an angel had spoken to him.

30Jesus said, 'This voice was for your benefit, not mine. 31Now is the time for judgment on this world; now the prince of this world will be driven out. 32But I, when I am lifted up from the earth, will draw all people to myself.' 33He said this to show the kind of death he was going to die.

34The crowd spoke up, 'We have heard from the Law that the Christ will remain for ever, so how can you say, "The Son of Man must be lifted up"? Who is this "Son of Man"?'

35Then Jesus told them, 'You are going to have the light just a little while longer. Walk while you have the light, before darkness overtakes you. Those who walk in the dark do not know where they are going. 36Put your trust in the light while you have it, so that you may become children of light.' When he had finished speaking, Jesus left and hid himself from them.

The Jews continue in their unbelief

37Even after Jesus had done all these miraculous signs in their presence, they still

A little while later, I asked God to forgive me for not living his way, and to help me to follow him in the future. At first, there wasn't an obvious difference in my life, as I was still fairly young at the time, but over the years I've been growing in my faith and God has always been there for me. The greatest proof of that came when I was fifteen and my mum died, after having been ill for several months with a heart condition. This came as an enormous shock, because I'd always believed she was going to get better and it was just a matter of finding the right drugs. In the immediate aftermath, I clung to God more than ever as someone I could rely on, and I found lots of love and support from my Christian friends. However, after a while, I started to have these nagging doubts. If God loves me so much, why did he let this happen to me? Why didn't he heal her, as I know he could have done? I still don't have the answers to these questions, and it really hurts to know that I will never see my mum again. But as I look back on the whole thing, I can see God was there with me all along.

Since I began studying medicine, I think I've grown even more as a Christian. There are so many wonderful opportunities to meet with others and to learn more about God. I'm not saying being a Christian has made my life a bed of roses; in some ways it would be easier just to go with the crowd. But I wouldn't have it any other way; there are many good things about living God's way now, and I know there will be even more in the future.

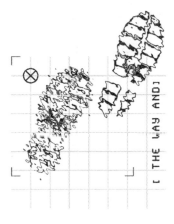

[THE WAY AND]

[48]

PROPHECY FULFILLED

John's concern is to demonstrate that the life and words of Jesus are not totally unexpected. Rather they fulfil predictions made through 2,000 years of Israel's history. Often John alludes only to earlier Jewish writings. But at this point he explicitly quotes from the prophet Isaiah's writings, penned about 700 years before Jesus Christ. Far from suddenly appearing unannounced on the pages of history, the life, words and death of Jesus Christ fit into a preconceived plan, promised by God through his messengers.

would not believe in him. 38This was to fulfil the word of Isaiah the prophet:

> 'Lord, who has believed our message
>> and to whom has the arm of the Lord been revealed?'

39For this reason they could not believe, because, as Isaiah says elsewhere:

40'He has blinded their eyes
>> and deadened their hearts,
> so they can neither see with their eyes,
>> nor understand with their hearts,
>> nor turn — and I would heal them.'

41Isaiah said this because he saw Jesus' glory and spoke about him.

42Yet at the same time many even among the leaders believed in him. But because of the Pharisees they would not confess their faith for fear they would be put out of the synagogue; 43for they loved human praise more than praise from God.

44Then Jesus cried out, 'Those who believe in me do not believe in me only, but in the one who sent me. 45When they look at me, they see the one who sent me. 46I have come into the world as a light, so that no-one who believes in me should stay in darkness.

47'As for those who hear my words but do not keep them, I do not judge them. For I did not come to judge the world, but to save it. 48There is a judge for those who reject me and do not accept my words; that very word which I spoke will condemn them at the last day. 49For I did not speak of my own accord, but the Father who sent me commanded me what to say and how to say it. 50I know that his command leads to eternal life. So whatever I say is just what the Father has told me to say.'

[4] Where am I heading?

'We live in a time of perfect means and confused ends.'
ALBERT EINSTEIN

'Men need a purpose which bears on eternity.'
MICHAEL POLANYI

'People bustle and strive and hurry. Their eyes are mostly on material considerations. They die, and apparently it's all over. What are we here for anyway? There must be some purpose in living, but I haven't found it yet. I'm restless and unhappy.'
NEW STUDENT

A question of purpose

Ralph Barton, the American satirical writer who committed suicide in 1931, wrote as an explanation for his death:'I have had few difficulties, many friends, great successes. I have gone from wife to wife, house to house, visited great countries of the world; but I am fed up with inventing devices to fill up 24 hours of the day.'[1]

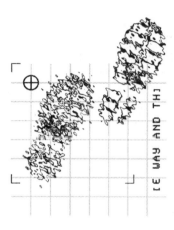

[49]

Chapters 13 – 17 record the last few tense hours Jesus spends with his followers before his trial and death (see chapters 18 – 19). Their sense of disorientation is reflected in their many questions. Jesus prepares them for his immediate departure, but also looks ahead to his life with them even after his death. He has plans that this small group of bewildered disciples should withstand times of vicious opposition, and begin to see others become his followers. His prayer in chapter 17 reflects his mission statement for his disciples.

CHAPTER [13]

Jesus washes his disciples' feet

¹It was just before the Passover Feast. Jesus knew that the time had come for him to leave this world and go to the Father. Having loved his own who were in the world, he now showed them the full extent of his love.

²The evening meal was being served, and the devil had already prompted Judas Iscariot, son of Simon, to betray Jesus. ³Jesus knew that the Father had put all things under his power, and that he had come from God and was returning to God; ⁴so he got up from the meal, took off his outer clothing, and wrapped a towel round his waist. ⁵After that, he poured water into a basin and began to wash his disciples' feet, drying them with the towel that was wrapped round him.

⁶He came to Simon Peter, who said to him, 'Lord, are you going to wash my feet?'

⁷Jesus replied, 'You do not realise now what I am doing, but later you will understand.'

Barton's words succinctly take us to the heart of the issue in this chapter. Life, if it is to be meaningful, has to be characterized by some sense of purpose. The tragedy of Barton's suicide was at one level simply the most logical outcome of his perception that his life had no purpose.

This is one of the very big questions, capable of keeping us and our friends up all night in frenzied discussion and argument. But it is none the less a question of fundamental importance. For as Lesslie Newbigin has put it: 'We have to act in order to live, and our actions will be determined by whether we believe the universe embodies a purpose other than our own or do not so believe. There is no third possibility.'[2] Moreover, it is clear that even the most heralded scientific breakthroughs will not in the end be able to answer our quest for answers. As Albert Einstein once wrote, science 'can teach us nothing beyond how facts are related to, and conditioned by, each other. The aspiration toward such objective knowledge belongs to the highest of which man is capable ... Objective knowledge provides us with the powerful instruments for the achievement of certain ends, but the ultimate goal itself and the longing to reach it must come from another source.'[3]

John's Gospel may rightly be said to be about a different kind of life, offered by Jesus Christ, which claims to be 'from another source'. Moreover, it is all about an answer to the quest for purpose. 'I have come', says Jesus, 'that they may have life, and have it to the full' (John 10:10). By this he means not only that he came to give us an outlook on life in this world that is transforming in its scope and vision, though he certainly does that. Leo Tolstoy – beginning the account of his own conversion – described the dramatic change it brought about in the following words:

[50]

⁸'No,' said Peter, 'you shall never wash my feet.'

Jesus answered, 'Unless I wash you, you have no part with me.'

⁹'Then, Lord,' Simon Peter replied, 'not just my feet but my hands and my head as well!'

¹⁰Jesus answered, 'Those who have had a bath need only to wash their feet; their whole body is clean. And you are clean, though not every one of you.' ¹¹For he knew who was going to betray him, and that was why he said not every one was clean.

¹²When he had finished washing their feet, he put on his clothes and returned to his place. 'Do you understand what I have done for you?' he asked them. ¹³'You call me "Teacher" and "Lord", and rightly so, for that is what I am. ¹⁴Now that I, your Lord and Teacher, have washed your feet, you also should wash one another's feet. ¹⁵I have set you an example that you should do as I have done for you. ¹⁶I tell you the truth, servants are not greater than their masters, nor are messengers greater than those who sent them. ¹⁷Now that you know these things, you will be blessed if you do them.

Jesus predicts his betrayal

¹⁸'I am not referring to all of you; I know those I have chosen. But this is to fulfil the scripture: "He who shares my bread has lifted up his heel against me."

¹⁹'I am telling you now before it happens, so that when it does happen you will believe that I am He. ²⁰I tell you the truth, whoever accepts anyone I send accepts me; and whoever accepts me accepts the one who sent me.'

²¹After he had said this, Jesus was troubled in spirit and testified, 'I tell you the truth, one of you is going to betray me.'

²²His disciples stared at one another, at a loss to know which of them he meant. ²³One of them, the disciple whom Jesus loved, was reclining next to him. ²⁴Simon Peter motioned to this disciple and said, 'Ask him which one he means.'

Five years ago I came to believe in Christ's teaching and my life suddenly changed; I ceased to desire what I had previously desired, and I began to desire what I formerly did not want. What had previously seemed to me good seemed evil, and what had seemed evil seemed good. It happened to me as it happens to a man who goes out on some business and on the way suddenly decides that the business is unnecessary and returns home. All that was on his right hand is now on his left, and all that was on his left hand is now on his right.[4]

But Jesus also invites us to enter into an experience of life which transcends even death. What is being offered by him is therefore 'life' in the fullest possible sense of the word: life without end. In fact, these two offers (of life to the full here on earth, and life beyond death) are integrally related to one another. They revolve around the central claim of John that in Jesus Christ we meet someone who not only personally demonstrated a quality of life that none of us will ever match, but who personally overcame the power and finality of death itself.

From this vantage point, the question of purpose takes on a whole new meaning.

Jesus and funerals

The story that John relates in chapter 11 takes us right to the heart of these issues.

Its opening sentences are somewhat bizarre. Jesus' close friend Lazarus is lying terminally ill in the village of Bethany, some two miles to the south-east of Jerusalem on the further slopes of the Mount of Olives. His sisters, Mary and Martha send word to Jesus, but he delays his arrival until Lazarus has been dead for four days. His reasoning for this delay is misunderstood by his friends, who must initially have taken heart from his comments (in 11:4), that Lazarus's sickness would not end in death. Then, after another

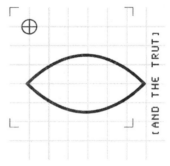

[AND THE TRUTH]

[51]

²⁵Leaning back against Jesus, he asked him, 'Lord, who is it?'

²⁶Jesus answered, 'It is the one to whom I will give this piece of bread when I have dipped it in the dish.' Then, dipping the piece of bread, he gave it to Judas Iscariot, son of Simon. ²⁷As soon as Judas took the bread, Satan entered into him.

'What you are about to do, do quickly,' Jesus told him, ²⁸but no-one at the meal understood why Jesus said this to him. ²⁹Since Judas had charge of the money, some thought Jesus was telling him to buy what was needed for the Feast, or to give something to the poor. ³⁰As soon as Judas had taken the bread, he went out. And it was night.

Jesus predicts Peter's denial

³¹When he was gone, Jesus said, 'Now is the Son of Man glorified and God is glorified in him. ³²If God is glorified in him, God will glorify the Son in himself, and will glorify him at once.

³³'My children, I will be with you only a little longer. You will look for me, and just as I told the Jews, so I tell you now: Where I am going, you cannot come.

³⁴'A new command I give you: Love one another. As I have loved you, so you must love one another. ³⁵By this everyone will know that you are my disciples, if you love one another.'

³⁶Simon Peter asked him, 'Lord, where are you going?'

Jesus replied, 'Where I am going, you cannot follow now, but you will follow later.'

³⁷Peter asked, 'Lord, why can't I follow you now? I will lay down my life for you.'

³⁸Then Jesus answered, 'Will you really lay down your life for me? I tell you the truth, before the cock crows, you will disown me three times!

misunderstanding – in which Jesus' reference to Lazarus 'sleeping' is taken as an encouragement by his friends, who assume that such rest will help him to recover – it transpires that his delay is specifically designed to allow Lazarus to die.

It must have been almost impossible for the disciples to keep up with a man who seemed to be compounding problems before meeting them: and then addressing those problems so majestically as to take their emotions from one end of the psychological spectrum to the other. No wonder John frequently draws attention to the disciples' inability to grasp what was really going on.

Jesus is indignant about death

John thus takes us into the narrative with a sense of expectation, alongside a certain bewilderment. Once Jesus arrives at the scene of the funeral, John takes us into hitherto unrecorded territory. For though he describes the emotional reactions of Lazarus's friends and family, our attention is held by his description of Jesus' own emotions.

Not only does he describe Jesus as weeping (11:35), but he also refers twice to the fact that Jesus is deeply and emotionally moved (even disturbed) by what is going on. When he sees the commotion of those around him, John says, Jesus 'was deeply moved in spirit and troubled' (11:33). Then as Jesus approaches the tomb, he is 'once more deeply moved' (11:38). The translators struggle to express the sense adequately here, for it is extremely forceful. The Greek word is used of horses when they 'snort' with indignation. One translator puts it: 'He gave way to such distress of spirit as made his whole body tremble …'[5]

But why the display of emotion on this scale? Perhaps it was because the bystanders appeared to lack the faith in his own promise to act. Certainly the weeping and wailing that surround the first occurrence might suggest this as a possibility. But it is difficult to

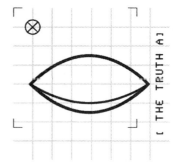

[THE TRUTH A]

[52]

CHAPTER [14]

Jesus comforts his disciples

[1]'Do not let your hearts be troubled. Trust in God; trust also in me. [2]In my Father's house are many rooms; if it were not so, I would have told you. I am going there to prepare a place for you. [3]And if I go and prepare a place for you, I will come back and take you to be with me that you also may be where I am. [4]You know the way to the place where I am going.'

Jesus the way to the Father

[5]Thomas said to him, 'Lord, we don't know where you are going, so how can we know the way?'

[6]Jesus answered, 'I am the way and the truth and the life. No-one comes to the Father except through me. [7]If you really knew me, you would know my Father as well. From now on, you do know him and have seen him.'

[8]Philip said, 'Lord, show us the Father and that will be enough for us.'

[9]Jesus answered: 'Don't you know me,

integrate this with the context of the second occurrence, where Jesus is approaching the tomb itself. The most likely explanation therefore is that it is the presence and devastation of death itself which evoke in Jesus this strong, convulsive reaction.

I suppose that at one level, we all share this strong reaction to the presence of death, particularly when it takes those we know and love, and removes them from us. For death renders us completely helpless. Perhaps because of this, our society has no real answers to the presence of death, and all we can do is to resign ourselves to its oncoming certainty – sooner or later. Our cultural attitudes towards it are therefore characterized perhaps most often by a consciously pursued ignorance. The American behavioural psychologist B. F. Skinner encouraged this line in an article some years back:

> What arouses fear is not death itself, but the act of talking and thinking about it, and that can be stopped. We brood about death when we have nothing else to do. The more reason we have to pay attention to life, the less time we have for attention to death. A properly executed will can give you the satisfaction of knowing your possessions will go to the right people, and you can extend the life of part of yourself by donating any organs that might still be useful. When these things have been done, it is probably better not to think about death.[6]

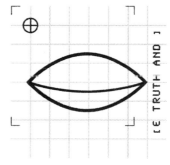

[53]

And when we have to address the issue, it is often humour that is used as a weapon against its potential seriousness. Woody Allen is famous for his slightly jaundiced attitudes on a number of issues, including death. In his play *Death*, he writes: 'It's not that I'm afraid to die: I just don't want to be there when it happens.' Yet the humorous façade conceals for Allen – as it does for so many – a far more serious fear, tinged perhaps with an inevitable helplessness. In an article for *Esquire* magazine entitled 'Woody Allen Wipes the

THE WORLD

'The world' is used in several senses in the book – one referring to the earth itself, or to people, the population of the earth. There is, however, another common meaning – society operating as if there is no God, or even opposing God. This shows itself in values which contradict God's, and in attitudes which are hostile to followers of Jesus. It is in this sense that Jesus views his followers as no longer being part of 'the world'. Although they remain on earth, they do not 'belong' in terms of life commitment.

Philip, even after I have been among you such a long time? Anyone who has seen me has seen the Father. How can you say, "Show us the Father"? 10Don't you believe that I am in the Father, and that the Father is in me? The words I say to you are not just my own. Rather, it is the Father, living in me, who is doing his work. 11Believe me when I say that I am in the Father and the Father is in me; or at least believe on the evidence of the miracles themselves. 12I tell you the truth, all who have faith in me will do what I have been doing, and they will do even greater things than these, because I am going to the Father. 13And I will do whatever you ask in my name, so that the Son may bring glory to the Father. 14You may ask me for anything in my name, and I will do it.

Jesus promises the Holy Spirit

15'If you love me, you will obey what I command. 16And I will ask the Father, and he will give you another Counsellor to be with you for ever — 17the Spirit of truth. The world cannot accept him, because it neither sees him nor knows him. But you know him, for he lives with you and will be in you. 18I will not leave you as orphans; I will come to you. 19Before long, the world will not see me any more, but you will see me. Because I live, you also will live. 20On that day you will realise that I am in my Father, and you are in me, and I am in you. 21Those who have my commands and obey them are the ones who love me. Those who love me will be loved by my Father, and I too will love them and show myself to them.'

22Then Judas (not Judas Iscariot) said, 'But, Lord, why do you intend to show yourself to us and not to the world?'

23Jesus replied, 'Those who love me will obey my teaching. My Father will love them, and we will come to them and make our home with them. 24Anyone who does not love me will not obey my teaching. These words you hear are not my own; they belong to the Father who sent me.

25'All this I have spoken while still with

Smile off his Face', he wrote that death 'is absolutely stupefying in its terror and it renders anyone's accomplishments meaningless'.[7] On another occasion he wrote, 'There will be no major solution to the suffering of mankind until we reach some understanding of who we are, what the purpose of creation was, what happens after death. Until these questions are resolved we are caught.'[8]

Two kinds of 'death'

But is Jesus' reaction here similar in kind to that of Woody Allen? Is it simply another human reaction to something which is ultimately beyond his control? Before we see what John has to say about this, it is important to say something about what the Bible more generally has to say about the reality of 'death'. For it actually speaks of *two* kinds of death, each of them involving some sort of separation. Physical death clearly separates the dead from the living, and is the immediate issue here for Lazarus's sisters and friends. For where there is death, there cannot be life, for death puts an end to it and removes a person from the sphere of physical life.

But there is another kind of death referred to in the Bible. We might call this 'spiritual' death. Like physical death, it too involves a separation. Just as those who are physically dead are cut off from the source of physical life, so those who are spiritually dead are cut off from the source of spiritual life: God himself. As a result they cannot experience the possibility of spiritual life that God intended all his creatures to enjoy. Existentially, the experience of spiritual death demonstrates itself in that spiritual search which never quite finds what it is looking for, or in that feeling that God is either unknown altogether, or appears to be far away from our experience and grasp.

But it is much more than simply an 'experience' in which we feel ourselves to be

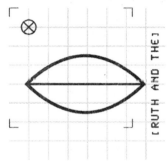

[TRUTH AND THE]

[54]

you. 26But the Counsellor, the Holy Spirit, whom the Father will send in my name, will teach you all things and will remind you of everything I have said to you. 27Peace I leave with you; my peace I give you. I do not give to you as the world gives. Do not let your hearts be troubled and do not be afraid.

28'You heard me say, "I am going away and I am coming back to you." If you loved me, you would be glad that I am going to the Father, for the Father is greater than I. 29I have told you now before it happens, so that when it does happen you will believe. 30I will not speak with you much longer, for the prince of this world is coming. He has no hold on me, 31but the world must learn that I love the Father and that I do exactly what my Father has commanded me.

'Come now; let us leave.

'searching for something' that is presently out of our reach. The New Testament writers put it far more seriously than that. We are under the sentence and experience of spiritual death because of a poison called 'sin', which infects our lives from top to bottom and makes us dead to God. 'The sting of death', writes the apostle Paul in the New Testament, 'is sin.'[9] The reason for this is that at its heart, 'sin' is the attitude of life whereby we turn our backs on God; in which each of us lives our life – with all its decisions, reactions, plans, ambitions, goals, hopes and fears – as if God has no right to be part of it.

As a result, we do not know him, for we are completely unable to relate to him. This second kind of death, therefore, has eternal consequences. For unless something is done about it, the God who is not known in the present will not be known in eternity. Our physical death will simply serve to confirm our spiritual death.

Spiritual death is therefore a great deal more subtle (and actually more serious) than physical death. It can often be easily dismissed or glossed over. After all, you can be spiritually dead whilst still being physically alive. Taking a walk down the High Street, you can normally tell who is physically dead and who isn't! Even in lectures, the living and the dead can normally be successfully distinguished. But whether people blink, talk or move is not an indication of whether they are spiritually alive to God.

Jesus and 'death'

To return to the story in chapter 11, when Jesus is described as being 'indignant' about death, he is reacting at least against death in its physical dimension. Death is seen by him as a kind of alien intruder into the ideal state of God's world. But John (with the rest of the New Testament writers) takes us further than this. For it becomes clear that Jesus is also incensed about the reality of 'spiritual' death as well. Moreover, his indignation at the

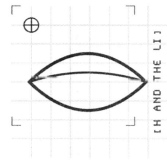

[55]

THE VINE

This is Jesus' final 'I am' saying recorded by John (see note on 'The "I am" sayings', 6:35). Jesus and his friends may have been passing a vine at this point. Behind Jesus' image stands a familiar historical idea of the Jewish nation as God's vine or vineyard. Jesus claims to be the genuine vine, unlike Israel, which sadly has failed to keep up its calling. The reference to pruning alludes to the testing time Jesus' followers are about to undergo.

CHAPTER [15]

The vine and the branches

¹'I am the true vine, and my Father is the gardener. ²He cuts off every branch in me that bears no fruit, while every branch that does bear fruit he prunes so that it will be even more fruitful. ³You are already clean because of the word I have spoken to you. ⁴Remain in me, and I will remain in you. No branch can bear fruit by itself; it must remain in the vine. Neither can you bear fruit unless you remain in me.

⁵'I am the vine; you are the branches. If you remain in me and I in you, you will bear much fruit; apart from me you can do nothing. ⁶If you do not remain in me, you are like a branch that is thrown away and withers; such branches are picked up, thrown into the fire and burned. ⁷If you remain in me and my words remain in you, ask whatever you wish, and it will be given you. ⁸This is to my Father's glory, that you bear much fruit, showing yourselves to be my disciples.

⁹'As the Father has loved me, so have I

graveside of Lazarus was not simply a helpless emotional gesture of sympathy. It is the springboard for a unique and majestic initiative.

In the first place, it led him to his own death. As we saw in more detail in chapter 4, this was no ordinary death. For at its heart John wants to tell us that this death has to be described in terms of God doing something on our behalf that we could not do ourselves. In possibly the most famous statement in the Bible, John has already said that 'God so loved the world that he gave his one and only Son, that whoever believes in him shall not perish but have eternal life' (3:16). How is this so? To continue with the 'sting' metaphor that we quoted earlier from one of Paul's letters, the death of Jesus can be described in terms of his taking into his own body the sting of sin and death, so that we need not suffer its ultimate poison ourselves. Imagine a parent who voluntarily takes the sting of a bee into his or her own body in order to protect a child from being stung. Now picture the sting as a poison that will separate us from God for all eternity. Replace the parent with Jesus Christ, and put yourself in the place of the child. This is the sort of picture that is being described in the pages of the Bible. Peter – one of Jesus' closest friends – puts it in this way in one of his New Testament letters: Jesus 'himself bore our sins in his body on the tree, so that we might die to sins and live for righteousness; by his wounds you have been healed.'[10]

Jesus demonstrates his authority over death

But not only does Jesus deal with death by his own crucifixion. He also demonstrates in the Lazarus episode that this victory over death is visibly complete. It covers both the spiritual and physical dimensions.

John paints the picture for us in primary colours by taking us right into the jaws of

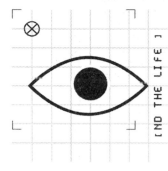

[AND THE LIFE]

[56]

loved you. Now remain in my love. ¹⁰If you obey my commands, you will remain in my love, just as I have obeyed my Father's commands and remain in his love. ¹¹I have told you this so that my joy may be in you and that your joy may be complete. ¹²My command is this: Love each other as I have loved you. ¹³Greater love has no-one than this, to lay down one's life for one's friends. ¹⁴You are my friends if you do what I command. ¹⁵I no longer call you servants, because servants do not know their master's business. Instead, I have called you friends, for everything that I learned from my Father I have made known to you. ¹⁶You did not choose me, but I chose you and appointed you to go and bear fruit – fruit that will last. Then the Father will give you whatever you ask in my name. ¹⁷This is my command: Love each other.

The world hates the disciples

¹⁸'If the world hates you, keep in mind that it hated me first. ¹⁹If you belonged to the world, it would love you as its own. As it is, you do not belong to the world, but I have chosen you out of the world. That is why the world hates you. ²⁰Remember the words I spoke to you: "Servants are not greater than their masters." If they persecuted me, they will persecute you also. If they obeyed my teaching, they will obey yours also. ²¹They will treat you this way because of my name, for they do not know the One who sent me. ²²If I had not come and spoken to them, they would not be guilty of sin. Now, however, they have no excuse for their sin. ²³Those who hate me hate my Father as well. ²⁴If I had not done among them what no-one else did, they would not be guilty of sin. But now they have seen these miracles, and yet they have hated both me and my Father. ²⁵But this is to fulfil what is written in their Law: "They hated me without reason."

²⁶'When the Counsellor comes, whom I will send to you from the Father, the Spirit of truth who goes out from the Father, he

death. Remember, we are at a funeral. Moreover, Lazarus has been in the tomb for four days (11:17). By this statement, John probably refers to the contemporary belief that a person's spirit 'hovered' over the body for up to four days before finally departing. So John here is emphasizing that – by any account – Lazarus is really and truly dead. Martha understandably therefore comments that if Jesus has the stone removed from the entrance to the tomb (as he is now proposing), there will be nothing but a dreadful stench (11:39). The repeated statement from both sisters to Jesus, 'If you had been here, my brother would not have died' (11:21 and 11:32), serves to emphasize both the fact that death had already taken place, and that attention is now increasingly being focused upon Jesus and what he may do.

What he does is beyond all expectations. Franco Zeffirelli had it about right in his film *Jesus of Nazareth*. Jesus summons Lazarus from the tomb with a word of command, and Lazarus slowly emerges into the bright daylight, shuffling because of the grave-clothes wound around his body. After the disbelief of the crowd has simmered down, Jesus (so down to earth – as he often is when he has done something so completely out of this world) suggests that they take off his grave-clothes and let him go (11:44).

Lazarus, Jesus and the 'death' thing

As we begin to pull out of this scene and view it with a wide-angle lens (so to speak), Jesus' actions in this chapter begin to take on even more radically significant and far-reaching proportions.

As if the miracle itself were not enough, John again wants to take the reader further. The observant will already have started to pick up the clues. This miracle is recorded by John as another of what he describes as 'signs' (see 12:17–18). In fact (excluding the

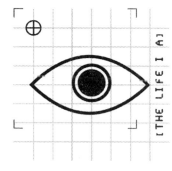

[THE LIFE I A]

[57]

will testify about me. [27]And you also must testify, for you have been with me from the beginning.

John 15:27

resurrection itself), it is the last that he records. As such, it works like the other 'signs' that he has written about in that the way that Jesus responds to the situation reveals something of God's glory.[11] But it also points beyond itself to an even deeper reality, a greater miracle, to which it is a signpost.

For whereas the miracle with Lazarus brought him back to the same kind of life he had previously known, the resurrection of Jesus is of a quite different order. John draws attention to this in interesting ways. Certainly, there was no 'calling out' of Jesus from the tomb. At least, not audibly. After all, what human being could have done it? When Jesus' friends Peter and John arrive at the tomb on the Sunday morning, they find it already empty. But it appears that there is something very odd about what has taken place. When Peter entered the tomb, he 'saw the strips of linen lying there, as well as the burial cloth that had been around Jesus' head. The cloth was folded up by itself, separate from the linen' (20:6–7).[12] Then the other disciple entered, and John writes simply that 'He saw and believed' (20:8). Suddenly, somehow, the piece of the jigsaw slots into place for him. Was it the fact that no grave-tamperer would have left the burial clothes lying around (especially with the head-piece folded)? We are not told specifically, but the writer certainly appears to be drawing a contrast with the story of Lazarus at this point. Lazarus could not have been separated from his grave-clothes even if he had wanted to be (which would have been difficult, being dead). No, the grave-clothes for Lazarus confirm the cosmic finality that death brings. They are his appropriate burial dress, and when he emerges, they have to be removed from him.

But for Jesus, things are radically different. He simply seems to have left his grave-clothes behind – neatly folded – as if they had just come back from the dry-cleaners. He has no need of them. They have nothing to do with him now, for (unlike those of Lazarus)

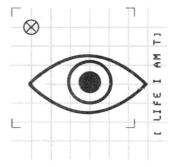

[LIFE I AM T]

[58]

When Jesus announced that he was leaving his followers, he met with disbelief and considerable sorrow. Their hopes had been pinned on him. He reassures them that he will not leave them unsupported but promises them another helper, the Holy Spirit. The Spirit would not be like some frightening apparition. He would enable them to understand Jesus and his ways even more clearly. Though Jesus would not be present physically, the Spirit would come alongside them to continue what he had been doing.

CHAPTER [16]

¹'All this I have told you so that you will not go astray. ²They will put you out of the synagogue; in fact, a time is coming when those who kill you will think they are offering a service to God. ³They will do such things because they have not known the Father or me. ⁴I have told you this, so that when the time comes you will remember that I warned you. I did not tell you this at first because I was with you.

The work of the Holy Spirit

⁵'Now I am going to him who sent me, yet none of you asks me, "Where are you going?' ⁶Because I have said these things, you are filled with grief. ⁷But I tell you the truth: It is for your good that I am going away. Unless I go away, the Counsellor will not come to you; but if I go, I will send him to you. ⁸When he comes, he will convict the world of guilt in regard to sin and righteousness and judgment: ⁹in regard to sin, because people do not believe in me; ¹⁰in regard to righteousness, because I am

they are simply not his appropriate dress. The reason for this is that Jesus is not being brought back to the life that he had previously known. Rather – in some extraordinary and unique way – he has passed through death and out the other side into a new kind of life. This new life is certainly physical, in the sense that his friends were able to recognize him. Thomas is actually invited to touch the scars that the wounds of crucifixion have left behind (20:27). But there is something more to Jesus' new existence than simply being bodily present. For he is able to appear inside a room before his friends, even when the doors to that room had been locked (20:19 and 20:26)! His presence therefore must be described as being in some sense physical, but it is much more than physical.

How do you begin to describe the implications of all this? For me, the words of the author of the famous Narnia books get somewhere near it. Referring to the resurrection, C. S. Lewis writes that Jesus 'has forced open a door that had been locked since the death of the first man. He has met, fought and beaten the King of Death. Everything is different because he has done so. This is the beginning of the New Creation. A new chapter in cosmic history has opened.'[13] Big words indeed, with cosmic implications. But how else do you begin to do justice to what John records in his Gospel? For Jesus shows his authority over death itself, in both its dimensions: physical and spiritual.

Jesus and the question of purpose

'It has never at any time been possible to fit the resurrection of Jesus into any world view except a world view of which it is the basis.' So wrote Lesslie Newbigin over thirty years ago.[14] And he was, of course, right. If the resurrection is true, it is the truth around which our world must now and for ever revolve. And once a person comes to base his or her life on its reality, then everything begins to be illuminated by a different light.

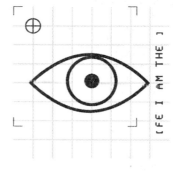

[59]

going to the Father, where you can see me no longer; [11]and in regard to judgment, because the prince of this world now stands condemned.

[12]'I have much more to say to you, more than you can now bear. [13]But when he, the Spirit of truth, comes, he will guide you into all truth. He will not speak on his own; he will speak only what he hears, and he will tell you what is yet to come. [14]He will bring glory to me by taking from what is mine and making it known to you. [15]All that belongs to the Father is mine. That is why I said the Spirit will take from what is mine and make it known to you.

[16]'In a little while you will see me no more, and then after a little while you will see me.'

The disciples' grief will turn to joy

[17]Some of his disciples said to one another, 'What does he mean by saying, "In a little while you will see me no more, and then after a little while you will see me," and "Because I am going to the Father"?' [18]They kept asking, 'What does he mean by "a little while"? We don't understand what he is saying.'

[19]Jesus saw that they wanted to ask him about this, so he said to them, 'Are you asking one another what I meant when I said, "In a little while you will see me no more, and then after a little while you will see me"? [20]I tell you the truth, you will weep and mourn while the world rejoices. You will grieve, but your grief will turn to joy. [21]A woman giving birth to a child has pain because her time has come; but when her baby is born she forgets the anguish because of her joy that a child is born into the world. [22]So with you: Now is your time of grief, but I will see you again and you will rejoice, and no-one will take away your joy. [23]In that day you will no longer ask me anything. I tell you the truth, my Father will give you whatever you ask in my name. [24]Until now you have not asked for anything in my name. Ask and you will

The question of 'purpose' that we have been considering in this chapter takes on a completely new perspective. Jesus shows us that views of life which are this-worldly and earthbound not only miss the point; they leave us spiritually dead and cut off from the source of true life. If therefore my aim in life is exclusively 'to pass my exams, get a good job, and then start raking the money in' (as someone said to me recently), then according to John, I will succeed only in losing my life. No, because of the resurrection of Jesus, true life is revealed as something different and more brilliant altogether.

That is why this chapter about Lazarus finds its climax in the words of Jesus to Martha: 'I am the resurrection and the life. Those who believe in me will live, even though they die; and whoever lives and believes in me will never die' (11:25–26).

Stop and think about these words. For, in effect, Jesus envelops both the future and the present in the brilliant light of his resurrection power. First the future. When he says, 'Those who believe in me will live, even though they die', he refers to the fact that even though we will all physically die one day, those who lean the weight of their lives upon Jesus Christ in trust and faith will never be separated from the life that God gives.

But this is not only a future promise. Jesus says that because of who he is, this truth can begin to take hold of our lives immediately: in the present. 'I am the resurrection … whoever lives and believes in me will never die.' At this moment, then, whoever you are, Jesus Christ invites you to enter a new life. We can know God's resurrection life now. Forgiven. Heading for heaven.

'Do you believe this?' he asks Martha (11:26). By extension, of course, John allows Jesus' question to be addressed via Martha to you, the reader – whoever you are. For this is why John wrote his Gospel in the first place. 'Jesus did many other miraculous signs in the presence of his disciples, which are not recorded in this book. But these are written that

[I AM THE TRU]

[60]

receive, and your joy will be complete.

²⁵'Though I have been speaking figuratively, a time is coming when I will no longer use this kind of language but will tell you plainly about my Father. ²⁶In that day you will ask in my name. I am not saying that I will ask the Father on your behalf. ²⁷No, the Father himself loves you because you have loved me and have believed that I came from God. ²⁸I came from the Father and entered the world; now I am leaving the world and going back to the Father.'

²⁹Then Jesus' disciples said, 'Now you are speaking clearly and without figures of speech. ³⁰Now we can see that you know all things and that you do not even need to have anyone ask you questions. This makes us believe that you came from God.'

³¹'You believe at last!' Jesus answered. ³²'But a time is coming, and has come, when you will be scattered, each to your own home. You will leave me all alone. Yet I am not alone, for my Father is with me.

³³'I have told you these things, so that in me you may have peace. In this world you will have trouble. But take heart! I have overcome the world.'

you may believe that Jesus is the Christ, the Son of God, and that by believing you may have life in his name' (20:30–31).

[R E A L   L I V E S]

L Y N D S E Y   M A R C H A M

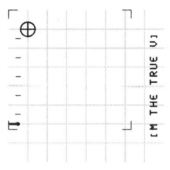

Lyndsey recently graduated with a degree in Law with French.

The first time I heard anything significant about God I was ten years old. I wasn't from a Christian family, and although I had been used to going to church occasionally, I thought that God was very distant.

But then a friend told me something about Jesus - that I needed his forgiveness. And as I got older, I met other Christians who told me the same thing. This made me quite angry. No-one was going to tell me I wasn't good enough for God; and I was sure that God couldn't be bothered about the things I had done wrong. But these people were different, and something about their love for each other, and even their love for God (who to me was quite far away) made me take them

[ʊ ƎUᴚ⊥ ƎH⊥ W]

GLORY

Glory, a significant word in John's vocabulary, links two ideas:

- the honour due to God: Jesus has 'glorified the Father', bringing honour to God by his life.
- the revealing of God's greatness: Jesus by his actions allows people to see the reality of the invisible God.

In his miracles especially, the greatness of God is allowed to shine. Jesus' death also reveals God's 'glory'. His suffering highlights the greatness of God's love for the world.

CHAPTER [17]

Jesus prays for himself

[1]After Jesus said this, he looked towards heaven and prayed:

'Father, the time has come. Glorify your Son, that your Son may glorify you. [2]For you granted him authority over all people that he might give eternal life to all those you have given him. [3]Now this is eternal life: that they may know you, the only true God, and Jesus Christ, whom you have sent. [4]I have brought you glory on earth by completing the work you gave me to do. [5]And now, Father, glorify me in your presence with the glory I had with you before the world began.

Jesus prays for his disciples

[6]'I have revealed you to those whom you gave me out of the world. They were yours; you gave them to me and they have obeyed your word. [7]Now they know that everything you have given me comes from you. [8]For I gave them the words you gave me and they

seriously. I went to some meetings, and talked to some Christian friends about what I should do, although I tried to do this without their realizing I was genuinely interested, because I was too embarrassed to admit openly that I'd been wrong! I even started reading the Bible.

I learned that instead of putting God at the heart of my life, I had prioritized myself - my own desires and ambition. Living such a life without God had made him angry - he had created me with loving care and rightfully demanded first place in my life. I was heading for the judgment I deserved in hell. This was serious.

What I needed more than anything was God's loving gift of forgiveness and new life that is offered only through Jesus - his death and resurrection -to stop being turned against God, and start living for him and with him. Gradually, I put my trust in Jesus. I was fourteen. So now I know that God's promises are true. He is no longer far away, but I know him every day in my life; praying to him and reading the Bible. In all the ups and downs of life I know that I have been rescued out of hell and, because of Jesus, I'll be where God is for ever - in heaven.

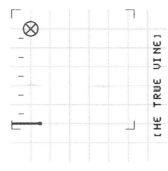

[THE TRUE VINE]

[62]

accepted them. They knew with certainty that I came from you, and they believed that you sent me. 9I pray for them. I am not praying for the world, but for those you have given me, for they are yours. 10All I have is yours, and all you have is mine. And glory has come to me through them. 11I will remain in the world no longer, but they are still in the world, and I am coming to you. Holy Father, protect them by the power of your name – the name you gave me – so that they may be one as we are one. 12While I was with them, I protected them and kept them safe by that name you gave me. None has been lost except the one doomed to destruction so that Scripture would be fulfilled.

13'I am coming to you now, but I say these things while I am still in the world, so that they may have the full measure of my joy within them. 14I have given them your word and the world has hated them, for they are not of the world any more than I am of the world. 15My prayer is not that you take them out of the world but that you protect them from the evil one. 16They are not of the world, even as I am not of it. 17Sanctify them by the truth; your word is truth. 18As you sent me into the world, I have sent them into the world. 19For them I sanctify myself, that they too may be truly sanctified

Jesus prays for all believers

20'My prayer is not for them alone. I pray also for those who will believe in me through their message, 21that all of them may be one, Father, just as you are in me and I am in you. May they also be in us so that the world may believe that you have sent me. 22I have given them the glory that you gave me, that they may be one as we are one: 23I in them and you in me. May they be brought to complete unity to let the world know that you sent me and have loved them even as you have loved me.

24'Father, I want those you have given me to be with me where I am, and to see my

[5] Where do I go from here?

What kind of response should the reader make to the Gospel of John, and its message about Jesus Christ? That is the question behind this last introductory section.

Perhaps you've read the Gospel itself and as a result have come to the point of acknowledging the need to do something with this person, Jesus.

Perhaps you simply want to know what it means to become a follower of Jesus.

Understanding the message

If you have read the Gospel itself, you will no doubt already have come across places where Jesus himself has made an invitation to you, the reader. Many of them have gathered around the so-called 'I am' sayings that he uses both to introduce himself and to describe in picture and metaphor how good it is to put our trust in him. Here are some examples:

> *I am the bread of life. Whoever comes to me will never go hungry, and whoever believes in me will never be thirsty.*
> JOHN 6:35

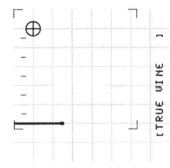

[63]

glory, the glory you have given me because you loved me before the creation of the world.

²⁵'Righteous Father, though the world does not know you, I know you, and they know that you have sent me. ²⁶I have made you known to them, and will continue to make you known in order that the love you have for me may be in them and that I myself may be in them.'

I am the light of the world. Whoever follows me will never walk in darkness, but will have the light of life.

JOHN 8:12

I am the good shepherd; I know my sheep and my sheep know me.

JOHN 10:14

I am the resurrection and the life. Those who believe in me will live, even though they die; and whoever lives and believes in me will never die.

JOHN 11:25–26

In other places, John himself seems to gather up the truth that he has been communicating about Jesus and put it into one place in a kind of summary. This method helps the reader to understand the different elements of the message and to grasp them as a coherent and succinct whole. A good example of this is in the passage 3:16–19, in which John effectively makes four statements about the Christian message:

[16]For God so loved the world that he gave his one and only Son, that whoever believes in him shall not perish but have eternal life. [17]For God did not send his Son into the world to condemn the world, but to save the world through him. [18]Those who believe in him are not condemned, but those who do not believe stand condemned already because they have not believed in the name of God's one and only Son. [19]This is the verdict: Light has come into the world, but people loved darkness instead of light because their deeds were evil.

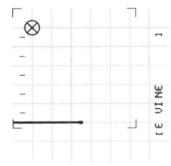

[64]

CHAPTER [18]

Jesus arrested

[1]When he had finished praying, Jesus left with his disciples and crossed the Kidron Valley. On the other side there was an olive grove, and he and his disciples went into it.

[2]Now Judas, who betrayed him, knew the place, because Jesus had often met there with his disciples. [3]So Judas came to the grove, guiding a detachment of soldiers and some officials from the chief priests and Pharisees. They were carrying torches, lanterns and weapons.

[4]Jesus, knowing all that was going to happen to him, went out and asked them, 'Who is it you want?'

[5]'Jesus of Nazareth,' they replied.

'I am he,' Jesus said. (And Judas the traitor was standing there with them.) [6]When Jesus said, 'I am he,' they drew back and fell to the ground.

[7]Again he asked them, 'Who is it you want?'

STATEMENT [1]

God loves the world and wants people to have eternal life.

For God so loved the world that he gave his one and only Son, that whoever believes in him shall not perish but have eternal life.

JOHN 3:16

First, this statement sums up God's attitude to the world of which you and I are a part. He loves it. Indeed, his creation of it was the expression of this love in action, and his creation of the human race was the pinnacle of that creative work. Moreover, God goes on expressing that love in a way that is neither removed nor distant. John's particular point here is that this love is great enough and deep enough to send God's one and only Son into the world as a human being. This is the greatest expression of his love for us.

Secondly, John tells us what God's purpose is in sending Jesus. It is, he says, that we might 'not perish but have eternal life'. This life – as we have seen – has two aspects to it. On the one hand, it has to do with a new dimension to our present lives. For to know God and to be known personally by God cannot fail to be anything less than what a friend of mine describes as 'living in an extra dimension'. It doesn't remove us from the problems and pressures, but enables us, through a personal relationship with God, to live through them and during them with a new understanding and a real hope.

But – as we have also seen – the life which Jesus came to bring is described as 'eternal', precisely because it will finally transcend even death. Death will not affect the relationship that believers have with God, for those who believe in Jesus Christ 'have crossed over from death to life' (5:24) and can never be separated from the life of God himself. The

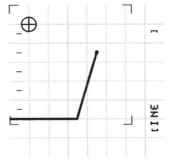

[65]

HIGH PRIEST

Throughout Israel's history a hereditary priesthood had operated, representing the people before God. The high priest had a special role among the priests, operating in both political and spiritual spheres. In the time of Jesus, the high priest had the power to collect taxes, represent the Jews in dealings with the Roman occupiers, supervise worship in the temple, and oversee the Sanhedrin (the supreme Jewish religious, political and legal council). Annas and Caiaphas, the former and current high priests respectively, played out their roles in the questioning of Jesus.

And they said, 'Jesus of Nazareth.'

8'I told you that I am he,' Jesus answered. 'If you are looking for me, then let these men go.' 9This happened so that the words he had spoken would be fulfilled: 'I have not lost one of those you gave me.'

10Then Simon Peter, who had a sword, drew it and struck the high priest's servant, cutting off his right ear. (The servant's name was Malchus.)

11Jesus commanded Peter, 'Put your sword away! Shall I not drink the cup the Father has given me?'

Jesus taken to Annas

12Then the detachment of soldiers with its commander and the Jewish officials arrested Jesus. They bound him 13and brought him first to Annas, who was the father-in-law of Caiaphas, the high priest that year. 14Caiaphas was the one who had advised the Jews that it would be good if one person died for the people.

Peter's first denial

15Simon Peter and another disciple were following Jesus. Because this disciple was known to the high priest, he went with Jesus into the high priest's courtyard, 16but Peter had to wait outside at the door. The other disciple, who was known to the high priest, came back, spoke to the female servant on duty at the door and brought Peter in.

17'You are not one of his disciples, are you?' she asked Peter.

He replied, 'I am not.'

18It was cold, and the servants and officials stood round a fire they had made to keep warm. Peter also was standing with them, warming himself.

The high priest questions Jesus

19Meanwhile, the high priest questioned Jesus about his disciples and his teaching.

20'I have spoken openly to the world,' Jesus replied. 'I always taught in synagogues or at the temple, where all the Jews come

resurrection of Jesus was a first demonstration or prototype of the resurrection that all who come to put their trust in him will one day experience.

This, then, is God's loving purpose for each and every one of us. It is an offer of life that is not only beyond compare: it is quite literally beyond this world. But the tragedy of our world is expressed in the next statement.

STATEMENT [2]

People show by their lives that they have rejected God.

This is the verdict: Light has come into the world, but people loved darkness instead of light because their deeds were evil.
JOHN 3:19

Our natural inclination as God's creatures, says John, is nevertheless (amazingly) to turn our backs on God and his purpose for our lives. It is to attempt to live as if none of this were true, and as though God himself did not even exist. The Bible calls this way of living sinful, and its central attitude of rejection 'sin'.

As a consequence, we do not naturally know what it is to have eternal life as the fundamental characteristic of our own lives. We live instead in what John describes as 'darkness': the vivid metaphor of what it means to reject God's light of life. Moreover, he says, we love this darkness. The reason for this is that since the things we do are signs of our moral rebellion against God, the exposure of these failures by the light of God's truth is too painful for many to face. In fact, says John, 'All those who do evil hate the light, and

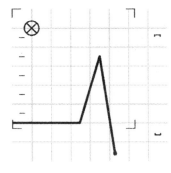

[66]

PILATE

Pontius Pilate, Roman governor of Judea from AD 26 to 36/7, had a reputation as both an able administrator and a harsh ruler. A contemporary described him as 'very merciless as well as very obstinate', reflecting his ruthless suppression of any Jewish uprising. In sentencing Jesus to death, Pilate acted partly out of fear of a potential riot, despite his repeated statement that the charges did not carry any weight. He is a sorry figure, caught between his conscience and the threats of the people.

together. I said nothing in secret. 21Why question me? Ask those who heard me. Surely they know what I said.'

22When Jesus said this, one of the officials near by struck him in the face. 'Is this the way you answer the high priest?' he demanded.

23'If I said something wrong,' Jesus replied, 'testify as to what is wrong. But if I spoke the truth, why did you strike me?' 24Then Annas sent him, still bound, to Caiaphas the high priest.

Peter's second and third denials

25As Simon Peter stood warming himself, he was asked, 'You are not one of his disciples, are you?'

He denied it, saying, 'I am not.'

26One of the high priest's servants, a relative of the man whose ear Peter had cut off, challenged him, 'Didn't I see you with him in the olive grove?' 27Again Peter denied it, and at that moment a cock began to crow.

Jesus before Pilate

28Then the Jews led Jesus from Caiaphas to the palace of the Roman governor. By now it was early morning, and to avoid ceremonial uncleanness the Jews did not enter the palace; they wanted to be able to eat the Passover. 29So Pilate came out to them and asked, 'What charges are you bringing against this man?'

30'If he were not a criminal,' they replied, 'we would not have handed him over to you.'

31Pilate said, 'Take him yourselves and judge him by your own law.'

'But we have no right to execute anyone,' the Jews objected. 32This happened so that the words Jesus had spoken indicating the kind of death he was going to die would be fulfilled.

33Pilate then went back inside the palace, summoned Jesus and asked him, 'Are you the king of the Jews?'

34'Is that your own idea,' Jesus asked, 'or did others talk to you about me?'

will not come into the light for fear that their deeds will be exposed' (3:20). People love darkness for what it conceals, and to allow the moral perfection of God's light to penetrate into our darkness is to invite the exposure of our real motives and desires.

So people naturally continue to live in a way that excludes God and invites condemnation and death. But what is God's own reaction to this fundamental rejection of him?

STATEMENT [3]

God still loves people and has sent Jesus to die so that they might be forgiven rather than condemned.

> *For God so loved the world that he gave his one and only Son, that whoever believes in him shall not perish but have eternal life. For God did not send his Son into the world to condemn the world, but to save the world through him.*
> JOHN 3:16–17

God's response to our rejection of him is not what you might expect. He has, of course, every right to reject us. For the way we live in his world with complete disregard for him is nothing short of scandalous. Imagine arriving home to find that intruders in your living-room have helped themselves to the contents of your fridge, and are living it up as if they owned your place. What would your reaction be? If you had the courage to express yourself in this situation, I'd guess that your comments would reflect your moral outrage. This is not their property; they have no right to treat it as if it was theirs; and you are now going to make sure that justice is done.

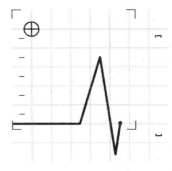

[67]

35'Am I a Jew?' Pilate replied. 'It was your people and your chief priests who handed you over to me. What is it you have done?'

36Jesus said, 'My kingdom is not of this world. If it were, my servants would fight to prevent my arrest by the Jews. But now my kingdom is from another place.'

37'You are a king, then!' said Pilate.

Jesus answered, 'You are right in saying I am a king. In fact, for this reason I was born, and for this I came into the world, to testify to the truth. Everyone on the side of truth listens to me.'

38'What is truth?' Pilate asked. With this he went out again to the Jews and said, 'I find no basis for a charge against him. 39But it is your custom for me to release to you one prisoner at the time of the Passover. Do you want me to release "the king of the Jews"?'

40They shouted back, 'No, not him! Give us Barabbas!' Now Barabbas had taken part in a rebellion.

But even though we do a similar thing as far as God is concerned (but on a far more serious scale, and with infinitely more serious consequences), God's extraordinary reaction to our indifference towards him is completely unlike our own reaction to those who treat us and our possessions in similar ways.

For instead of rejecting us out of hand, or handing us over to the kind of justice which would be our inevitable fate, he takes the initiative to reconcile us to himself. By sending his Son Jesus into the world to be crucified, he provides the means by which you and I can be forgiven. 'God did not send his Son into the world to condemn the world,' says John, 'but to save the world through him' (3:17).

On the cross Jesus himself willingly took upon himself the condemnation for our rebellion against God that should have been ours, so that we might be spared that condemnation and saved from its finality. As the early church writer Tertullian puts it simply: 'He came for this purpose, that he himself, free from all sin, and altogether holy, should die for sinners.'[1]

STATEMENT [4]

There will always be one of two responses to this news.

Those who believe in him are not condemned, but those who do not believe stand condemned already because they have not believed in the name of God's one and only Son.

JOHN 3:18

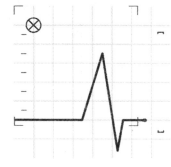

[68]

CHAPTER [19]

Jesus sentenced to be crucified

[1]Then Pilate took Jesus and had him flogged. [2]The soldiers twisted together a crown of thorns and put it on his head. They clothed him in a purple robe [3]and went up to him again and again, saying, 'Hail, king of the Jews!' And they struck him in the face.

[4]Once more Pilate came out and said to the Jews, 'Look, I am bringing him out to you to let you know that I find no basis for a charge against him.' [5]When Jesus came out wearing the crown of thorns and the purple robe, Pilate said to them, 'Here is the man!'

[6]As soon as the chief priests and their officials saw him, they shouted, 'Crucify! Crucify!'

But Pilate answered, 'You take him and crucify him. As for me, I find no basis for a charge against him.'

[7]The Jews insisted, 'We have a law, and according to that law he must die, because he claimed to be the Son of God.'

[8]When Pilate heard this, he was even more afraid, [9]and he went back inside the

There have only ever been two possible responses to this message about Jesus that John has told us. People either receive it in humility and with a profound sense of thankfulness, or else they persist in rejecting it.

But the common idea that there is some neutral territory that people are now occupying, which is neither for nor against God, is a figment of the imagination. People say: 'I'm going to wait until later in life – until things have calmed down a bit – to decide about Jesus Christ.' They may believe that until that moment of decision they are in a morally neutral zone, in which they haven't decided one way or another and therefore cannot really bear responsibility. But John says here that those who do not believe 'stand condemned already because they have not believed'. There are no fences in this business. It is not a case of opting into faith or opting into unbelief. There were only ever two categories: belief and disbelief. So If I have not yet responded to the light of Jesus and have not believed in the rescue mission that God accomplished through him, I am in darkness, and – says John – under God's present condemnation.

But, John continues – and it's the best 'but' possible – if I believe in Jesus Christ I will not be condemned. The act of believing who Jesus truly is, and trusting what he did for me, is the way out of condemnation. As Jesus himself says: 'I tell you the truth, those who hear my word and believe him who sent me have eternal life and will not be condemned; they have crossed over from death to life' (5:24).

Responding to the message

All through John's Gospel (as well as in the chapters I have written) we have come across the phrases 'believing in Jesus', or 'trusting' in him and what he has done. As we saw in the introductory chapter, this is not essentially a matter of assenting intellectually either to

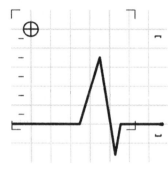

[69]

Death on a cross was a humiliating and cruel form of execution. The very public humiliation began when the victim was stripped naked. The ridicule continued as he was forced to carry to the place of execution the wooden beams to which he would soon be nailed through the wrists and ankles. The beams were then raised upright. A lingering death ensued, the whole process deliberately maximizing the torture. John spares us the gruesome details. He focuses on the reality of Jesus' death, and the way in which it fulfilled earlier predictions.

John 19:10–22

palace. 'Where do you come from?' he asked Jesus, but Jesus gave him no answer. [10]'Do you refuse to speak to me?' Pilate said. 'Don't you realise I have power either to free you or to crucify you?'

[11]Jesus answered, 'You would have no power over me if it were not given to you from above. Therefore the one who handed me over to you is guilty of a greater sin.'

[12]From then on, Pilate tried to set Jesus free, but the Jews kept shouting, 'If you let this man go, you are no friend of Caesar. Anyone who claims to be a king opposes Caesar.'

[13]When Pilate heard this, he brought Jesus out and sat down on the judge's seat at a place known as the Stone Pavement (which in Aramaic is Gabbatha). [14]It was the day of Preparation of Passover Week, about the sixth hour.

'Here is your king,' Pilate said to the Jews.

[15]But they shouted, 'Take him away! Take him away! Crucify him!'

'Shall I crucify your king?' Pilate asked.

'We have no king but Caesar,' the chief priests answered.

[16]Finally Pilate handed him over to them to be crucified.

The crucifixion

So the soldiers took charge of Jesus. [17]Carrying his own cross, he went out to the place of the Skull (which in Aramaic is called Golgotha). [18]Here they crucified him, and with him two others – one on each side and Jesus in the middle.

[19]Pilate had a notice prepared and fastened to the cross. It read: JESUS OF NAZARETH, THE KING OF THE JEWS. [20]Many of the Jews read this sign, for the place where Jesus was crucified was near the city, and the sign was written in Aramaic, Latin and Greek. [21]The chief priests of the Jews protested to Pilate, 'Do not write "The King of the Jews", but that this man claimed to be king of the Jews.'

[22]Pilate answered, 'What I have written, I have written.'

who Jesus is, or to what he has done. It is more a matter of responding with the will and the heart to what we are discovering. Of course, the mind has been involved. After all, John has been telling us that Christian faith is not about leaping into the dark, but out of it.

So as you have been reading and thinking about what John has been saying, a process of assimilation has been undoubtedly taking place. Like a child edging his or her way along the branch of a tree, intellectual progress is a process in which we subconsciously begin to assent to new discoveries in a way that enables us to put our weight on these things and move on a little in our pursuit of further truth. This happens in all branches of knowledge, not least in Christianity.

But as far as Christian faith is concerned, this knowledge is inescapably personal. It has to do with Jesus Christ, and all knowledge about God is personally mediated by him. As we have seen, Christian faith is about relating to Jesus as God in a way that brings the benefits of all that he offers into the orbit of our own personal lives. You will doubtless have felt the personal implications of what Jesus has been saying as you have read John's Gospel. You may have rejected these, or glossed over them, but they have been there nevertheless.

But maybe you have come to a particular consciousness that Jesus is addressing you. Perhaps you are uncomfortable about what he may think of you, but hopeful in view of his promise of safety and salvation. If this is the case, then – as with any personal friendship offered to you – the way to respond is to open up the conversation. We relate by talking. If John's Gospel is a 'word from God', what would you now like to say to him in reply?

[70]

There will be many things, of course, and, for the Christian, the life of prayer that faith opens up is the lifelong opportunity to talk with God about our concerns and desires, our hopes and fears. But to start this process, we need to speak with him for the first time.

Jesus' last words before his death do not simply mean he is resigned to his fate. Rather, it is a declaration of completion. In John's record, the whole life of Jesus is related to promises made throughout Israel's history. Jesus consciously fulfilled God's purpose in his life and also in his death. His cry 'It is finished' is a positive affirmation that he has fully accomplished God's will. His death is not an unexpected defeat but a climax. His resurrection would confirm the implied ultimate triumph.

23When the soldiers crucified Jesus, they took his clothes, dividing them into four shares, one for each of them, with the undergarment remaining. This garment was seamless, woven in one piece from top to bottom.

24'Let's not tear it,' they said to one another. 'Let's decide by lot who will get it.'

This happened that the scripture might be fulfilled which said,

'They divided my garments among them
and cast lots for my clothing.'

So this is what the soldiers did.

25Near the cross of Jesus stood his mother, his mother's sister, Mary the wife of Clopas, and Mary Magdalene. 26When Jesus saw his mother there, and the disciple whom he loved standing near by, he said to his mother, 'Dear woman, here is your son,' 27and to the disciple, 'Here is your mother.' From that time on, this disciple took her into his home.

The death of Jesus

28Later, knowing that all was now completed, and so that the Scripture would be fulfilled, Jesus said, 'I am thirsty.' 29A jar of wine vinegar was there, so they soaked a sponge in it, put the sponge on a stalk of the hyssop plant, and lifted it to Jesus' lips. 30When he had received the drink, Jesus said, 'It is finished.' With that, he bowed his head and gave up his spirit.

31Now it was the day of Preparation, and the next day was to be a special Sabbath. Because the Jews did not want the bodies left on the crosses during the Sabbath, they asked Pilate to have the legs broken and the bodies taken down. 32The soldiers therefore came and broke the legs of the first man who had been crucified with Jesus, and then those of the other. 33But when they came to Jesus and found that he was already dead, they did not break his legs. 34Instead, one of the soldiers pierced Jesus' side with a spear, bringing a sudden flow of blood and water. 35The man who saw it has given

In doing so, I suggest that we need to cover the areas that were covered in the four statements above.

- We need to thank God for his purpose for our lives expressed in the coming of Jesus.

- We need to say how sorry we are for the fact that we have lived in the rejection of this purpose.

- We need to thank God for sending Jesus to save us from condemnation.

- We need to ask for God's forgiveness and for his help in responding to him and living for him from now on.

You may like to use the words below.

```
Dear God
Thank you that your purpose for my life is that I may know
'eternal life'. I am so sorry for the ways in which I have
rejected your love expressed in the coming of Jesus. But thank you
that you still love me - enough to send Jesus to die so that I may
be forgiven and not condemned. Please forgive me now and help me
to live for you as my Saviour and King from now on.
Amen.
```

If you have prayed this prayer, why not tell another Christian so that he or she can help you to go on from here?

testimony, and his testimony is true. He knows that he tells the truth, and he testifies so that you also may believe. ³⁶These things happened so that the scripture would be fulfilled: 'Not one of his bones will be broken,' ³⁷and, as another scripture says, 'They will look on the one they have pierced.'

The burial of Jesus

³⁸Later, Joseph of Arimathea asked Pilate for the body of Jesus. Now Joseph was a disciple of Jesus, but secretly because he feared the Jews. With Pilate's permission, he came and took the body away. ³⁹He was accompanied by Nicodemus, the man who earlier had visited Jesus at night. Nicodemus brought a mixture of myrrh and aloes, about seventy-five pounds. ⁴⁰Taking Jesus' body, the two of them wrapped it, with the spices, in strips of linen. This was in accordance with Jewish burial customs. ⁴¹At the place where Jesus was crucified, there was a garden, and in the garden a new tomb, in which no-one had ever been laid. ⁴²Because it was the Jewish day of Preparation and since the tomb was near by, they laid Jesus there.

[REAL LIVES]

JOVAN SANKER

Jovan is in the midst of her studies in Economics and Management at Balliol College, Oxford.

I was very fortunate to have been brought up in a Christian home back in Trinidad where I come from. I was taught from an early age that Jesus Christ was the way, the truth and the life, but there came a time when I had to think for myself and make my own response. So, even though I knew that God loved me, and I was called to love and serve him in return, my appetite for a relationship with him really started to grow when I entered the Sixth Form.

Since then, there has been no turning back. I know that everything I've accomplished has been due to him, and he really is the centre of my joy. My friends can't understand why I'm always joyful - one of them even complains that's it's unnatural. But how can I not be happy when the creator of the universe sacrificed himself for me, lives within me, meets every one of my needs, and loves me with an unconditional love that no human brain can ever truly fathom? How can I not be happy when Jesus is at the heart of my life every day and cares for me always?

[72]

CHAPTER [20]

The empty tomb

[1]Early on the first day of the week, while it was still dark, Mary Magdalene went to the tomb and saw that the stone had been removed from the entrance. [2]So she came running to Simon Peter and the other disciple, the one Jesus loved, and said, 'They have taken the Lord out of the tomb, and we don't know where they have put him!'

[3]So Peter and the other disciple started for the tomb. [4]Both were running, but the other disciple outran Peter and reached the tomb first. [5]He bent over and looked in at the strips of linen lying there but did not go in. [6]Then Simon Peter, who was behind him, arrived and went into the tomb. He saw the strips of linen lying there, [7]as well as the burial cloth that had been around Jesus' head. The cloth was folded up by itself, separate from the linen. [8]Finally the other disciple, who had reached the tomb first, also went inside. He saw and believed. [9](They still did not understand from Scripture that Jesus had to rise from the dead.)

I know this must sound like blind faith to those who are not Christians, but it is much more that that. It's a conviction that the one whom I serve is the true and living God, that his will is holy and perfect, and that from my own experience, I can find fullness of joy and a peace of mind beyond comprehension in him. My life is fearless despite the struggles I've faced and will continue to face, and I exist according to Philippians 4:13: 'I can do everything through him [Christ] ...'

Since coming to Oxford, my love for Jesus Christ has grown enormously, as well as my ability to trust him with everything that concerns me. From things like adjusting to a new country and choosing the right church, to my relationships, friendships and academic and social commitments, he has proved yet again how well he can sustain me. My life is victorious because of him. I hope you choose to share in that victory too.

Jesus appears to Mary Magdalene

¹⁰Then the disciples went back to their homes, ¹¹but Mary stood outside the tomb crying. As she wept, she bent over to look into the tomb ¹²and saw two angels in white, seated where Jesus' body had been, one at the head and the other at the foot.

¹³They asked her, 'Woman, why are you crying?'

'They have taken my Lord away,' she said, 'and I don't know where they have put him.' ¹⁴At this, she turned round and saw Jesus standing there, but she did not realise that it was Jesus.

¹⁵'Woman,' he said, 'why are you crying? Who is it you are looking for?'

Thinking he was the gardener, she said, 'Sir, if you have carried him away, tell me where you have put him, and I will get him.'

¹⁶Jesus said to her, 'Mary.'

She turned towards him and cried out in Aramaic, 'Rabboni!' (which means Teacher).

¹⁷Jesus said, 'Do not hold on to me, for I have not yet returned to the Father. Go instead to my brothers and tell them, "I am returning to my Father and your Father, to my God and your God."'

¹⁸Mary Magdalene went to the disciples with the news: 'I have seen the Lord!' And she told them that he had said these things to her.

Jesus appears to his disciples

¹⁹On the evening of that first day of the week, when the disciples were together, with the doors locked for fear of the Jews, Jesus came and stood among them and said, 'Peace be with you!' ²⁰After he said this, he showed them his hands and side. The disciples were overjoyed when they saw the Lord.

²¹Again Jesus said, 'Peace be with you! As the Father has sent me, I am sending you.' ²²And with that he breathed on them and said, 'Receive the Holy Spirit. ²³If you forgive the sins of anyone, their sins are forgiven; if you do not forgive them, they are not forgiven.'

[Notes]

Introduction

1 The noun 'truth' occurs fifty-two times in John's twenty-one chapters.

[1] Where do I start?

1 Douglas Coupland, *Life after God* (London: Simon & Schuster, 1994), pp. 273–274.

2 Quoted from Bertrand Russell's *Autobiography* by R. MacKenna, *God for Nothing* (London: Souvenir Press, 1984), p. 56.

3 Graham Ward, *The Postmodern God* (Oxford: Blackwell, 1997), pp. xv–xvi.

4 *The Observer*, November 1993.

Jesus appears to Thomas

24Now Thomas (called Didymus), one of the Twelve, was not with the disciples when Jesus came. 25So the other disciples told him, 'We have seen the Lord!'

But he said to them, 'Unless I see the nail marks in his hands and put my finger where the nails were, and put my hand into his side, I will not believe it.'

26A week later his disciples were in the house again, and Thomas was with them. Though the doors were locked, Jesus came and stood among them and said, 'Peace be with you!' 27Then he said to Thomas, 'Put your finger here; see my hands. Reach out your hand and put it into my side. Stop doubting and believe.'

28Thomas said to him, 'My Lord and my God!'

29Then Jesus told him, 'Because you have seen me, you have believed; blessed are those who have not seen and yet have believed.'

30Jesus did many other miraculous signs in the presence of his disciples, which are not recorded in this book. 31But these are written that you may believe that Jesus is the Christ, the Son of God, and that by believing you may have life in his name.

5 C. S. Lewis, Letter to Arthur Greeves (11 December 1944) in *They Stand Together* (London: Collins, 1979), p. 503.

6 From a sermon Bonhoeffer preached in Barcelona, 1928. Quoted in E. Bethge, *Dietrich Bonhoeffer* (London: Fount, 1977), p. 84.

7 The origin of the term 'docetist' is from the Greek *dokeo*, to 'seem' or 'appear' to be something.

8 For example, in Paul's letter to the Romans (8:5).

9 Quoted in L. Osborn, *Angels of Light?* (London: Darton Longman & Todd, 1992), p. 188.

10 Coupland, *Life after God*, p. 359.

[2] Who am I?

1 Peter Berger, *Invitation to Sociology: A Humanistic Perspective* (Harmondsworth: Penguin, 1966), p. 109.

2 Quoted in M. Wroe, *God: What the Critics Say* (London: Spire, 1992), p. 7.

3 Quoted in J. R. Middleton and B. J. Walsh, *Truth is Stranger than it Used to be* (London: SPCK, 1995), pp. 52–53.

4 Zygmunt Bauman, *Postmodernity and its Discontents* (Cambridge: Polity Press, 1997), p. 178.

5 Augustine, *Confessions*, Book 1:1 (Harmondsworth: Penguin, 1961), p. 21.

6 Pascal, *Pensées* 131 (Harmondsworth: Penguin, 1966), p. 65.

7 John frequently uses the word 'hour' or 'time' to refer to Jesus' coming death (e.g. 2:4; 7:30; 8:20; 12:23, 27; 13:1).

8 Pascal, *Pensées* 417, p. 148.

9 Peter Berger, Brigitte Berger and Hansfried Kellner, *The Homeless Mind: Modernization and Consciousness* (Harmondsworth: Penguin, 1973), p. 74.

Simon Peter had been a leading follower of Jesus for about three and a half years. His severely strained loyalty eventually gave way during Jesus' trial (18:15–27). He adamantly denied any connection with Jesus three times, underscoring the extent of his desertion. Jesus' treatment of Peter following his resurrection is not to sideline but to reinstate him. He forces Peter to face his failure by echoing his three-fold denial with three questions, but clearly he still has a place for him in his plans.

CHAPTER [21]

Jesus and the miraculous catch of fish

[1]Afterwards Jesus appeared again to his disciples, by the Sea of Tiberias. It happened this way: [2]Simon Peter, Thomas (called Didymus), Nathanael from Cana in Galilee, the sons of Zebedee, and two other disciples were together. [3]'I'm going out to fish,' Simon Peter told them, and they said, 'We'll go with you.' So they went out and got into the boat, but that night they caught nothing.

[4]Early in the morning, Jesus stood on the shore, but the disciples did not realise that it was Jesus.

[5]He called out to them, 'Friends, haven't you any fish?'

'No,' they answered.

[6]He said, 'Throw your net on the right side of the boat and you will find some.' When they did, they were unable to haul the net in because of the large number of fish.

[7]Then the disciple whom Jesus loved said to Peter, 'It is the Lord!' As soon as Simon Peter heard him say, 'It is the Lord,' he wrapped his outer garment around him

[4] Where am I heading?

1 Quoted in Mark McCloskey, *Tell it Often, Tell it Well* (San Bernardino: Here's Life, 1985), p. 95.

2 Lesslie Newbigin, *Proper Confidence* (London: SPCK, 1995), p. 58.

3 Albert Einstein, *Ideas and Opinions* (London: Souvenir Press, 1973), p. 42.

4 Leo Tolstoy, *What I Believe* (London: Oxford University Press, 1921).

5 J. B. Phillips' translation.

6 B. F. Skinner, 'In His Own Words', *People* magazine, 28 November 1983, p. 22.

7 *Esquire* magazine, May 1977, p. 72.

8 Quoted in M. Wroe, *God: What the Critics Say* (London: Hodder, 1992), p. 29.

9 Paul, in his first letter to the Corinthian believers (1 Corinthians 15:56).

10 In Peter's first letter (1 Peter 2:24).

11 See the comment in 2:13 after the first of the seven 'signs' that John records in chapters 2–11, as well as the comments of Jesus at the start of the Lazarus story (11:4).

12 Unlike that of Lazarus, which is still wound around his head (11:44).

13 C. S. Lewis, *Miracles* (London: Bles, 1947), p. 173.

14 Leslie Newbigin, *Honest Religion for Secular Man* (London: SCM, 1966), p. 53.

[5] Where do I go from here?

1 Tertullian, *De Pudicitia* 22.

JOHN'S PURPOSE

John does not write his account of Jesus' life simply as a biographer seeking to bring an objective, detached view of his main character. He makes no attempt to keep his agenda hidden. His bias does not mean he invents stories or glosses over the truth. Rather, he selects material from what he witnessed directly over three years (20:30–31). As (probably) Jesus' closest friend during that time, he is well placed to do so. He had observed him at close quarters. In presenting the character of Jesus, he wants us to piece together the evidence he has provided.

(for he had taken it off) and jumped into the water. [8]The other disciples followed in the boat, towing the net full of fish, for they were not far from shore, about a hundred yards. [9]When they landed, they saw a fire of burning coals there with fish on it, and some bread.

[10]Jesus said to them, 'Bring some of the fish you have just caught.'

[11]Simon Peter climbed aboard and dragged the net ashore. It was full of large fish, 153, but even with so many the net was not torn. [12]Jesus said to them, 'Come and have breakfast.' None of the disciples dared ask him, 'Who are you?' They knew it was the Lord. [13]Jesus came, took the bread and gave it to them, and did the same with the fish. [14]This was now the third time Jesus appeared to his disciples after he was raised from the dead.

Jesus reinstates Peter

[15]When they had finished eating, Jesus said to Simon Peter, 'Simon son of John, do you truly love me more than these?'

'Yes, Lord,' he said, 'you know that I love you.'

Jesus said, 'Feed my lambs.'

[16]Again Jesus said, 'Simon son of John, do you truly love me?'

He answered, 'Yes, Lord, you know that I love you.'

Jesus said, 'Take care of my sheep.'

[17]The third time he said to him, 'Simon son of John, do you love me?'

Peter was hurt because Jesus asked him the third time, 'Do you love me?' He said, 'Lord, you know all things; you know that I love you.'

Jesus said, 'Feed my sheep. [18]I tell you the truth, when you were younger you dressed yourself and went where you wanted; but when you are old you will stretch out your hands, and someone else will dress you and lead you where you do not want to go.' [19]Jesus said this to indicate the kind of death by which Peter would glorify God. Then he said to him, 'Follow me!'

JOHN'S PURPOSE

John's encounter with Jesus Christ was a life-changing experience for John, and he wants a similar one for us. This person, John tells us, is not just another human being. He cannot be explained simply as an outstanding teacher or faith-healer. John wants us to move beyond mere interest in Jesus' work and teaching. Understanding who Jesus really is, and believing in him, brings life (20:31). (See also notes on 'Messiah', 4:25, and on 'Life', 3:16.)

²⁰Peter turned and saw that the disciple whom Jesus loved was following them. (This was the one who had leaned back against Jesus at the supper and had said, 'Lord, who is going to betray you?') ²¹When Peter saw him, he asked, 'Lord, what about him?'

²²Jesus answered, 'If I want him to remain alive until I return, what is that to you? You must follow me.' ²³Because of this, the rumour spread among the believers that this disciple would not die. But Jesus did not say that he would not die; he only said, 'If I want him to remain alive until I return, what is that to you?'

²⁴This is the disciple who testifies to these things and who wrote them down. We know that his testimony is true.

²⁵Jesus did many other things as well. If every one of them were written down, I suppose that even the whole world would not have room for the books that would be written.